THE CONSULTANT'S MANUAL

THE CONSULTANT'S MANUAL

A Complete Guide to Building a Successful Consulting Practice

THOMAS L. GREENBAUM

JOHN WILEY & SONS, INC.

New York • Chichester • Brisbane • Toronto • Singapore

Library of Congress Cataloging-in-Publication Data

Greenbaum, Thomas L.
  The consultant's manual: a complete guide to building a
successful consulting practice / Thomas L. Greenbaum.
       p.   cm.
  Includes bibliographical references.
  ISBN 0-471-50119-0 (cloth)   ISBN 0-471-00879-6 (paper)
  1. Consultants—Handbooks, manuals, etc.   2. Consultants—
Marketing—Handbooks, manuals, etc.   I. Title.
HD69.C6G7   1989
001—dc20   89-36303
                                                 CIP

To Rosalie,
my wife and very best friend

Foreword

Over the years, I have had many occasions to use the services of small-to medium-size consulting firms. I have also known many consultants who entered this field because they felt they had the necessary talent and background to assist others in the development and growth of their businesses. As with most businesses, consultants create needs and market their talents in a highly competitive marketplace where the selection most often is made on a subjective basis. Once selected, however, the consultant must not only deliver results but must also prove to the client that it is worth their while to maintain this relationship because the consultant offers a service that will be beneficial to the growth of the company. To me, maintaining client relations is not only the most difficult part of the consulting business, but also the most important in establishing a successful and prosperous practice. Otherwise, the consultant finds that most of his or her time is being spent finding new clients to replace those who are leaving, and that one is waging a constant battle simply to maintain the businesss rather than growing it.

In *The Consultant's Manual*, Tom Greenbaum presents a comprehensive analysis of what a consultant needs to know to establish and market a practice effectively. Unlike most books that have been written on the subject, it is light on theory and concentrates primarily on being a working guide for a consultant who wants ultimately to build a business and grow revenues by offering a meaningful and desired service for clients.

Tom is eminently qualified to write this book because of his practical background and his teaching experience. He has spent more than twenty years in the consulting field, most recently as a founding partner of the Connecticut Consulting Group. For the past five years, he has taught a course at Harvard in which aspiring consultants from virtually every discipline have come to learn how to generate leads, sell their services, and finally, build their practices into profitable enterprises.

Regardless of whether a consultant intends to have a one-person operation or a larger, more comprehensive firm, this book contains all the vital information he or she will need. It is also extremely frank in its appraisal of how a consultant should behave in situations where many times the right answer is one the client may not want to hear. I have known Tom Greenbaum for over ten years, and he has always operated under the premise that one's integrity should be more important than making the client feel good for the moment. Perhaps that is the reason he has built a successful company and is recognized as one of the best teachers of the subject. It is also the reason I feel that Tom's book will become the definitive manual for people seeking to build a consulting practice.

Alan Pesky
Former Vice Chairman & COO, Scali, McCabe, Sloves, Inc.
Presently Chairman & CEO, Peak Media, Inc.

Stamford, Connecticut
November, 1989

Acknowledgments

This book never would have been completed without the involvement and encouragement of some people who have been very important to me.

First, my wife, Rosalie, and my two sons, Jeff and David, were always in the background cheering me on while I was writing. Even when it felt like the typing would never stop, the interest they showed in the project always seemed to be the spark that kept me going. I can't count the number of times my eleven-year-old son, David, would say "Well, Dad, how's the book coming?" a question that could appear at virtually any time. This was the secret ingredient that kept me plugging along.

Second, I find it most pleasurable to acknowledge once again the one person who has meant more to me than any other in my business career, Elaine Shepherd. My secretary and administrative assistant for sixteen years, she has performed many different tasks in a most outstanding manner. I could not imagine an individual more professional in her chosen field. She typed every word of this book and always provided helpful hints as the chapters were developed. Without her, there would have been no book. Of this I am sure.

Thirdly, I would like to thank all my clients over the past sixteen years, as each of them has contributed something special to this book. I have enjoyed so many of the relationships and have been so stimulated by the challenge of the assignments that it would be impossible to single out any particular individual or company. However, I am sure that those of you who were integral to my success as a consultant know who you are. To you all, I offer my sincerest thanks.

Finally, I want to thank Dr. David Campbell, Director of the Center for Lifelong Learning at Harvard University. David gave me the opportunity to teach in his department in 1984, and I have thoroughly enjoyed the opportunity of serving the university since that time. I have met some very interesting students and have been gratified by the correspondence that I have received from them months and years after they attended my course.

THOMAS L. GREENBAUM

New Canaan, Connecticut

Contents

Introduction

This book is about building and marketing a consulting service. This is a type of marketing that I believe is among the most difficult. It has been my experience that selling consulting services is difficult because in many (if not most) situations, one is selling a relatively expensive product, which is intangible and often difficult to describe, to an individual who frequently has a relatively undefined need. Moreover, all of this is accomplished without any guarantee of success for the buyer as a result of the purchase.

In the ideal world, an effective consultant would simply provide a superior product or service, and word would spread to the appropriate people about the outstanding capabilities of the individual or the consulting organization. As a result of this, the telephone would ring constantly, and the consultant would select the best clients to serve. However, this ideal world exists for only a select few. The rest of the consulting world must take positive action to generate new clients or submit to the deafening silence of waiting for potential clients to call.

It has been said many times that nothing happens until someone sells something. Certainly, this is true in the consulting business, as you do not become a consultant until an agreement for your services is established. Here, the statements "you get what you pay for" and "one who gives free advice often gives no advice" come into play. Many consultants have found that, though the conclusions and recommendations they provide their clients are no different from those developed (essentially for free) by the internal corporate staff several months earlier, their information has greater value because it comes from the outside paid consultant. People are much more likely to follow the advice of another person if they have paid that individual for his or her opinion.

The objective of this book is to provide you with tools that will help you build your business. While reading this book, constantly ask yourself the question, "Does this information apply to my type of consulting?" Consulting is a broad profession, involving a large number of different disciplines, each with its own cultures; all of the methods and techniques presented here will not be appropriate for every type of consultant. Still I can assure you that you will find sufficient relevant information to help you build a consulting business, regardless of the type of consulting service you offer.

This book is divided into two major sections, each of which is designed to achieve a different objective.

The first part of the book is about *planning*. It addresses the important issues that a consultant must face when deciding to enter the business and discusses the options available with regard to the different ways to get started. Importantly, it provides a review of the advantages and disadvantages associated with each alternative. Specifically, this part of the book will cover:

1. *The key elements of the business plan for a consulting practice.* The business plan is essential for any consulting organization, even if the intent of the practice is always to be a one-person business. This section provides a brief overview of the topics that should be covered in a business plan, with specific suggestions concerning the process of writing the plan for the consulting practice.

2. *The key issues that relate to establishing the structure of a consulting business.* What functions must be fulfilled, and how can they be handled in a small practice, using both internal and external resources?

3. *The importance of defining the scope of your consulting practice and why it is equally important to define the business you are **not** in.* This part of the book provides some very useful tips as to how to think about your consulting practice and how you can develop an effective definition of your business.

4. *The development of a positioning for your consulting practice.* This section defines positioning in the marketing plan and provides an approach to the identification of a viable positioning for the business.

5. *The determination of the target audience for your practice.* This portion of the book discusses how to identify your target audience and how to define this group in such a way that it will be effective in the overall marketing-plan implementation process.

6. *The choice of a name for your consulting practice.* This section covers the important issues that must be considered when selecting your company name, with an emphasis on strategy development, candidate name identification, and options available to the business that will contribute to determining the final name.

7. *The financial considerations that you should understand when planning your consulting practice.* This contains information about the development of forecasts of revenues, operating budgets, and the importance of cash flow when considering the start-up and ongoing operation of a consulting business. An integral part of this section deals with setting fees, providing a framework by which a consulting organization can determine what to charge for its services.

The second part of the book deals with *implementation*, specifically, the execution of the business plan. The quality of the execution of a business plan normally will be the most important factor in the success of a consulting business. The best plans will not work if they are not executed effectively, whereas even a relatively weak plan may succeed if the execution is flawless. This part of the book discusses the following major topics:

1. *Methods of building awareness of your consulting practice.* This provides a detailed overview of both direct and indirect methods of building awareness and discusses the advantages and disadvantages of each.

2. *The establishment of a sales culture in the organization.* This section of the book describes determining the role of sales in the

consultant's marketing plan, defining the sales process, and preparing for selling situations. It also discusses the elements of a sales presentation, the consultant's proposal, what it is and how it should be written, and how to handle common objections that arise in the selling of consulting services.

3. *The nature and role of customer service in the development and marketing of a consulting business.* This section surveys the most important aspects of customer service and identifies what the dimensions of service should (and should not) be in a typical service business.

4. *The corporate brochure.* This section examines the issues that should be addressed to determine whether you need a brochure and, if so, what type of brochure would be the appropriate for your practice. This part of the book also describes a suggested process for developing a brochure internally and points out some of the key questions that a small consulting practice should consider if it decides to hire an outside organization to write and produce the brochure.

5. *The ethics of the consulting business.* This last chapter deals with the need for a strong sense of ethics in the business, focusing on what types of actions a service organization should consider relative to ethical questions/issues.

This is not the type of book that you should read cover to cover like a novel; rather, it should first be skimmed and then read on a section-by-section basis as a guide during the process of planning and executing a marketing program. I strongly recommend that you begin by reviewing the early chapters that provide the theoretical background for the development of your business plan. Then, as actual program implementation commences, you will find the material in each of the chapters that cover the individual topic areas useful both as a resource for determining the content of the plan and as a source of ideas as to the specific elements that you feel are most appropriate for inclusion into your plan.

Part 1
Planning

1 Marketing Your Consulting Service

Virtually everyone who enters the consulting business faces the same two basic challenges; how to generate leads and then how to turn leads into clients. If a consultant does an effective job of planning the practice he is starting and then understands what is involved in marketing the practice to the appropriate parties, the probability of a success is extremely high.

Effective planning and flawless execution of the marketing of a consulting practice are integral to the overall philosophy behind this book. Throughout the years of teaching the course upon which this book is based, I often have been asked why this philosophy is not defined in terms of selling, advertising or promoting your consulting services. I settled on "marketing" because of the scope of the activities that are needed to develop a successful consulting practice. For example, selling your consulting services (discussed in great detail in Chapter 10) clearly is a very important—some say the most important—part of building a consulting business, and, for many consultants, it is the most difficult aspect of the business-building program. However, it is only one element of the overall program, which will not be effective without the employment of all the others.

Similarly, advertising or promotion frequently is the primary focus of the business building program for a new consulting practice. In many (if not most) such situations, the business building efforts begin with a major effort by the consultant to develop a company/practice logo and a brochure. In a large number of start-up consulting practices, there is a feeling that once a brochure has been developed, the marketing job is over, and all they have to do is gain reasonable distribution of the new advertising piece and then sit back to wait for the phone to ring.

Consultants who place their emphasis on either the advertising or promotion aspects of building the practice are approaching the business-building activities in a very limiting manner. Like selling, both advertising and promotion have an important role in any effort to develop a consulting practice, but they, too, are only pieces of the whole effort. You can do an excellent job of advertising or promoting your consulting practice, but if your services are not priced properly, sold correctly, and serviced effectively, it is highly unlikely that your business will ever be successful.

"Marketing" is the appropriate focus of this book because it encompasses all the activities needed to build a practice. More than advertising, more than promotion, and more than sales, marketing relates to them all and to a great many more things that will be discussed in detail in this book. An understanding of all of the elements of marketing—what is called "the Marketing Mix"—is crucial to the individual who is seeking to build an effective consulting practice.

THE MARKETING MIX

In 1964, the *Harvard Business Review* published a landmark article entitled "The Concept of the Marketing Mix." In this article, Harvard professor Neil Borden coined the term "marketing mix" to describe the variety of different marketing elements that must be "mixed" together to produce an effective marketing plan. These elements are often referred to as the "4 Ps": product, price, place, and promotion. Yet, while the 4 Ps clearly are germane for planning a marketing program for products such as soap, soft drinks, or salad dressings, it has been my experience that, in the consulting business, the elements become more numerous. I have developed a special consulting marketing mix which I call THE NINE Ps OF MARKETING A CONSULTING SERVICE (see Figure 1.1).

The consultants' marketing mix can be visualized as a bicycle wheel: The successful practice is the axle, and the various parts of the mix are the spokes. For the wheel to turn, each of the spokes must contribute to

Figure 1.1 The Consultant's Marketing Mix: The Nine Ps.

the functioning of the whole. If one spoke is weak, the wheel will not work effectively to propel the axle forward. The key to successful marketing of a consulting practice is to ensure that all elements of the mix are developed carefully and working at peak effectiveness.

The elements of the consultants' marketing mix are, briefly described, as follows:

  1. *Planning.* This consists of setting the direction for your business. For example, you should conduct some research to establish a description of the people who are most likely to use (purchase) your services, the needs and the wants of these potential buyers, and the most effective ways to deliver a convincing message to your target customers. You should determine the financial elements of the business such as revenue and expense forecasts, cash flow estimates, source of business analyses, and so on. You should also identify the most appropriate structure for the organization for both the short and longer term. Finally, you should consider such things as the number of people in the practice, the functions of the various personnel, and the likely flow of people (by function) in the organization.

2. *Price.* This element relates to the fee structure that you adopt for your practice. It includes not only how much is charged for your services but how you implement the fee structure. For example, will you base your fees on time incurred at a predetermined rate? On an assessment of the value of the service to the customer? On the competitive environment in which you are operating? Or will you base them on some other formula which seems to work best for you?

3. *Place.* This element of the mix refers to the location of your business in terms of such things as where it is geographically and how you will deliver your services to your clientele. For example, will you operate all services out of one office or have satellite facilities that are closer to your clients?

4. *Packaging.* This refers to the look of the consulting practice—the graphics of the stationery, business cards, and brochures, the decor of the company offices, and esthetic concerns in general.

5. *Positioning.* The positioning of the consulting practice establishes how you want your business to be viewed by the client/prospect population. In essence, the positioning is the personality and character of the business.

6. *People.* The people element of the mix refers to the types of clientele that the consulting practice is seeking to attract and the quality of the personnel in the practice.

7. *Product.* The product of the consulting practice consists of the services that your organization will offer your clients. This relates to the benefit that the client will receive as a result of hiring your consulting organization. In most marketing programs, the benefits normally are stated in terms of the features that are provided—the people in the organization, their professional credentials, and the types of projects that the practice offers—as it is easier to describe such generic attributes than to define the specific benefits that your clients will receive.

8. *Promotion.* This element incorporates the four key traditional marketing functions:

   Advertising. Advertising includes all the options available to the consulting organization, from standard media advertising (i.e., newspaper, magazine, radio, or television) to such things as Yellow Page ads, advertising specialties that incorporate the company name (pens, key chains, etc.), and other similar types of communications.

Promotion. Promotion includes any paid program that goes directly to the target consumer to stimulate interest in the consulting practice. An example would be a direct-mail program.

Public relations. Public relations is the use of unpaid media to generate awareness of the practice. This typically involves programs to interest third-party media (newspaper, television, magazines, radio) in doing stories about the practice.

Sales. This function is the process of selling your consulting services, including preparation for the sales call, execution of the sales presentation, development of the proposal, and the follow-up that is required after the call.

9. *Professionalism.* The professionalism of a consulting practice refers to such things as how the people in the practice relate to clients and suppliers, the activities in which your organization might wish to become involved within both the professional and the local community in which you operate, and the ethical standards by which your organization operates on a day-to-day basis.

2 Should You Enter the Consulting Business?

As you read this book, you may not yet have started a consulting practice. You may be working at another job, unemployed or simply in between jobs, or in school about to enter the job market. If so, there are some very important decisions that should be considered before entering the consulting business.

IS CONSULTING THE RIGHT CAREER FOR YOU?

In my experience, people enter the consulting business for one or more of the following reasons:

1. They are unemployed (or between jobs) and need something to do while they seek new positions. Some of these people stay in the profession, but the majority eventually return to the type of work they did before. These people have the opportunity to try consulting at a relatively low risk time in their careers: If they are successful, they can stay with it; if it does not work, many will still find the experience worthwhile, and they certainly will be no worse off than they were when they started.

2. They are attracted by the independence of consulting. It is a profession where they can be their own boss, working only the hours and times that suit their needs. If this is important to a prospective consultant, then the profession might be right for him or her.

3. They find the glamour and prestige of the business appealing— the idea of functioning as a high-level advisor to very senior executives is very attractive.

4. They have unique skills that they feel are marketable and would prefer to offer these capabilities to organizations on a contract rather than an employee basis.

While these may all be legitimate reasons for entering the consulting business, I believe that the people who identify closely with the last motivation have the greatest probability of success. The following criteria for success in the consulting business will help you to determine the extent to which you can relate to each of the areas.

A Marketable Skill

The most important factor you should consider when planning to enter the consulting business is the skill or technical expertise you can offer a prospective client. Are you just another smart person who wants to be a consultant? Or do you have a special skill, area of expertise, or unique experience that would be attractive to the types of people/organizations to whom you will seek to sell your services? You should not attempt to begin a consulting practice until you can answer this second question in the positive. Further, you must be able to define your skill in such a way that a prospective client will understand it easily.

A Very Strong Work Ethic

With very few exceptions, building a consulting business is a very difficult task that requires hard work, perseverance, and a strong desire to succeed. Unless you enter the business with a very well-known name, an established reputation, and a large number of potential client contacts, building a consulting business will be a challenge requiring a significant personal commitment.

Self-Motivation

Particularly in a small practice, successful consultants must be able to manage effectively their own time on a day-to-day basis. They must be people who operate on internal deadlines based on the needs of the assignment. These people do not have to write down project deadlines; they have an instinct for when things need to be done. One of the keys to success in the consulting business is reliability, in terms of delivering a quality project on time and on budget. Self-motivation is crucial to reliability.

Satisfaction With One's Own Work

I have found that long-term happiness in the consulting business derives from satisfaction with one's own work, regardless of whether others recognize the value of what has been accomplished. A consultant is expected to do excellent work all the time; if your job satisfaction depends on receiving plaudits from clients, you probably will not be very happy in consulting. This is not to suggest that clients do not praise good consulting work; they simply do not feel the need to do so as much as they might with an employee. Happy consultants are those who can recognize the quality of their own work and gain satisfaction from a job well done, with or without recognition from clients.

No Need for Total Control Over People or Programs

Consultants want to see their programs implemented by clients. However consultants can only recommend a course of action to their clients and hope that they will be able to sell the client on implementing it. They frequently have no control over the resources to manage the program execution. Some consultants become unhappy with this role because clients do not do everything they propose. It is my strong feeling that the happy consultant is the individual who develops the best possible program for the client, works hard to convince them to implement the recommendations, but does not take it as a personal or professional insult if the program is not implemented precisely as proposed or, in many cases, not executed at all, for a variety of reasons.

Excellent Written and Verbal Skills

In most types of consulting, communication with the client is a vital part of the product being sold. The way one communicates, on paper and/or in a stand-up presentation, can be a very important part of the sale to the client, both to establish the relationship and to get the developed programs implemented.

Strong Problem-solving/Analytical Abilities

In many, if not most, situations, a consultant is called into an organization because a problem needs to be solved. Often the problem is not well defined, and the client expects the consultant to help pinpoint the nature of the problem and then to propose the appropriate solution. This requires someone who is comfortable entering very unstructured situations and is able to determine what factors are germane to the problem at hand, so that progress toward a solution can be made.

WHAT OPTIONS ARE AVAILABLE WHEN YOU ENTER THE BUSINESS?

Once you have decided to enter the consulting business, you must make a few key follow-up decisions that will have a significant impact on the development of your personal career plan. Should you go into the business full-time or begin it as a part-time venture until you know that it will be successful? Should you start the business alone, or would you be better off finding a partner (or two)? Should you enter the business on your own or with a partner or get started in another organization, with the objective of venturing out into your own practice at a later date?

Start Off Full-time Versus Part-time

A great many people face the part-time/full-time decision as they consider entering the consulting business. In most situations, there are primarily two reasons for even considering this alternative. First, you may want to minimize the financial risks associated with a start-up consulting venture. Many people cannot or do not want to suffer the inevitable financial hardships of starting a business. Therefore, they begin by consulting on a part-time basis, in the evening, on weekends, or for a few days a week before they set aside their current source of income in order to consult full-time. Second, many people do not want to make a commitment to consulting until they are sure that it is something they want to do on a permanent basis.

Both of the above are legitimate considerations, but you should also consider the advantages and disadvantages associated with each option.

If you choose part-time consulting, you will minimize the financial risk associated with entering the business, as you will not have to relinquish your basic income to begin your practice. You will also be able to walk away from the business with minimal implications if you discover that it is not a desirable career option, or if you simply are not able to develop a sufficiently large practice to make the business a viable long-term economic proposition.

If you opt instead for full-time consulting, you will have a greater chance of success because consulting will be your sole source of income, and your motivation to seek new clients aggressively will be much greater. If you consult only part-time, on the other hand, it is easy to make consulting the second priority when things get busy at your basic job. There is also a very different emotional commitment to the business when you enter on a full-time basis. If you can focus all your mental energy on building the business and producing the best possible consulting product, the probability that this will happen is greater. With a full-time commitment to the business, you send a very different message to potential clients than would be the case with a part-time consulting practice. In most cases, prospective clients are much more receptive to working with people/organizations with a full-time commitment to the profession than with those that are consulting in their spare time.

A full-time commitment to consulting also offers the advantage of providing much quicker feedback about both the financial and the emotional benefits that you will get from the consulting business. In a full-time situation, you probably will know whether consulting is the right business for you in the first six months or year, whereas, in a part-time venture, it could take much longer for you to establish this.

Finally, in some consulting practices, a full-time commitment to the business may offer important competitive advantages that could be lost in a part-time practice. If you have a special skill, a unique experience, or some other highly marketable talent that is not currently available from other consultants, you might be able to use that advantage to your benefit. For example, an individual who has acquired special expertise during the early days of a new computer technology or gained experience in dealing with new laws that relate to bank regulation might have the opportunity to capitalize on this uniqueness because of the intense interest in the area among the target audience. If the practice is not full-time, however, the individual may not be able to benefit from the existing market conditions and could lose the competitive advantages that have been generated.

Begin the Company Alone or with a Partner or Partners

One of the most common questions typically raised by a person planning to start a consulting practice is whether to start alone and bring others into the business when it becomes more developed or to begin with one or more partners and build the practice together. There are very definite advantages to both approaches.

The biggest advantage to starting the business alone is that the person who begins the business is the boss and can easily justify being the major (or sole) owner for many years to come. This offers the possibility of very significant financial reward. In addition, a sole owner can structure the business in the way he or she wants, installing the systems and procedures that seem best for the company. This will form the overall strategic posture for the business. And, some people feel that one of the biggest advantages of starting the business alone is that it places increased pressure on the entrepreneur to make the practice successful, since there is no one else to blame if the business does not get off to a strong start.

Still, a great many entrepreneurially oriented people would not consider beginning a consulting practice alone, despite the obvious financial and control advantages. To these people, starting a consulting business with another individual provides a support system during the early days of the business when things might be very slow. A support system can be very reassuring and serve to boost overall morale significantly. A business with more than one principal also can leverage the contacts of both people to the benefit of the practice. If one of the principals is not having a successful time with his sales efforts, he might be able to assist the other and help to generate business from his prospects. Moreover, many clients feel that a consulting organization with more than one founding principal is more likely to deliver a higher-quality product, as the work benefits from the inputs of more senior/experienced people. Such a consulting practice is more saleable to new clients. Finally, many feel that starting a consulting business with more than one owner enables the key people to share the administrative workload. Since a company of two (or even more) people has virtually the same amount of administrative paperwork as a company of one, a joint start-up will enable the principals to focus more time on selling the services that will build the practice rather than on handling relatively nonproductive paperwork.

Start Out on Your Own or Join Another Organization First

Most people who consider opening their own consulting businesses are very negative about the concept of starting out by working for another company, with the objective of beginning their own venture in the future. There, however, some very significant advantages associated with working for someone else for some period of time before establishing your own consulting business. By beginning with someone else, you will develop business contacts that could be important sources of business when you go out on your own. You will have the opportunity to learn the consulting business (at least as someone else operates it) before beginning your own practice. This offers some meaningful benefits, as you will have a much better appreciation for the issues that need to be addressed when you begin to plan your own consulting business. You will learn *how* to be a consultant. Independent consulting is quite different from doing a similar job on the client side, and it is very important to learn certain aspects of the business, such as the key elements of client service, methods of prospecting for new business, the most effective ways to collect data during client assignments, and expense control and project time management. Another advantage of working for a consulting company before you establish your own practice, is that you are exposed to in-house systems and controls that you can later adapt easily to your new business. Developing these things from scratch would take a great deal of time, and you probably would have a long wait before these elements of the business were as effective as they could or should be.

Yet, beginning a consulting business without first working for someone else has its own advantages. Starting on your own enables you to begin your business immediately, when your level of enthusiasm is high, rather than waiting a year or more to begin this process. By starting alone, you do not risk being turned off about the business because of some specific company policies, procedures, politics, or other similar things in the temporary organization. And some people feel that, until you begin a business of your own, you will not know how effective you can be, as the motivation for success is not as great when you work for another person as it would be when your personal practice is at stake.

Now that you have made the decision to enter the consulting business, it is time to address the planning activities that you will need to implement in order to increase your chances of success in this new venture. The balance of this book assumes that you are planning to start your own consulting company, rather than work for someone else. The material will focus on providing you with the information you need to plan and then implement a marketing program for your practice.

3 The Business Plan

A business plan establishes the overall direction for your practice over the next one to three years. It functions much like a road map. Just as you could get from New York to Phoenix simply by driving west and then going south, you can succeed without a business plan. However, in both instances, the likelihood (and speed) with which you achieve your objectives increases dramatically when you have a well-thought out plan and execute it flawlessly.

WHY SHOULD YOU WRITE A BUSINESS PLAN?

There are several very important reasons why you should develop a business plan, even if your intent is always to operate as a one-person practice. A business plan will help you to define the direction of the business, in terms of what types of consulting the practice does and does not do. While this may appear to be very basic, it is particularly important as you are seeking to establish your practice. Defining the scope of your consulting practice will allow you to evaluate client opportunities objectively, to ensure that they are strategically correct for the business in light of your goals. A formal business plan also forces you to think through the key elements necessary to start and run your business (i.e., financial aspects, sales requirements, etc.) and to build and service a client base (i.e., manpower needs, systems, etc.). If you do not address these issues in a formal plan, you might forget about aspects of the program that could be vital to the success of the business. An effective business plan can also play an extremely important role in your dealings with the financial community. Often it will be the key factor that determines whether or not you obtain financing and, if so, how much money the bank will provide and at what rate of interest. Finally, the plan is an informational resource for potential employees or owners/operators of the business. When prospective employees consider joining a small business, one of their first questions will relate to the overall mission of the company and the plans for the future. While the owner can communicate this verbally, normally a formal document is more effective—plans seem more real when they are written down.

Under ideal circumstances, you should finish the planning part of your business (i.e., the *formal* business plan) at least six to eight weeks before you begin your practice, so that you will have time to complete the preliminary tasks indicated by the plan, such as the development of a new business presentation, the creation of a brochure, the design of a company logo, business cards, and stationery, the development of a prioritized hit list of prospective clients, and the composition of announcement letters, press releases, and other similar materials important to the start-up of a new organization. None of these elements of your marketing program can be completed until you have established the strategic direction and positioning for the organization.

A great many organizations that develop a business plan feel that their formal planning responsibilities are over once the entity is a going concern. Thenceforward, these organizations do their planning on the back of an envelope, focusing more on the numbers they plan to generate than on the strategic aspects of the business. This is *not* the intent of the business planning process, nor is it in the best long-term interests of your organization.

The best-run consulting organizations will make a commitment to the planning process which will continue even after the business begins. These organizations will update the plan annually to review where the business has gone in the previous year and to ensure that the goals and objectives that have been established for the coming year are realistic in light of the various elements of the marketing mix for the business.

WHAT SHOULD A BUSINESS PLAN CONTAIN?

The following outline describes the sections that should be included in all business plans, although the specific content of your business plan will vary according to the nature of your consulting practice. Most organizations likely will add other sections that relate directly to the unique aspects of their business.

1. *An overview of the market.* The opening section of the business plan should provide a brief overview of the business you are entering, specifically:

    a. A definition of the category or business in which the consulting practice will be operating. For example, if you are starting a consulting business in package design, this section would define what is meant by package design, in terms of the specific services your organization will provide to its clients in this area.

    b. An assessment of the size of the category and the growth trends in recent years. Some people are very intimidated by this task because they cannot provide accurate estimates of the size of the category. However, precision is not necessarily important here; rather, the intent is to provide the reader of the plan with some sense of whether the category is relatively large or small, new or old, growing or declining. Naturally, the more specific detail that you can include in the section, the better the plan, but the most important thing is to give some notion of the parameters of the market.

    c. An assessment of the environment in which the new company will be competing. This should include a description of the major competitors in the business, with brief biographical sketches of the most important competitors.

2. *A statement of the key success criteria for the business.* This section of the plan is intended to indicate the most important aspects of success for the type of consulting business being formed. Typical subjects normally included in this section might include the following:

    a. The need to build a relatively large staff quickly, in order to reach a level where the company can service a wide variety of client needs effectively

    b. The need to have a large number of small clients (as opposed to a small number of larger clients) because of the frequent turnover of relationships and the dangers inherent in being dependent upon a very small number of clients for company revenues

    c. The need to operate at very high margin levels in order to avoid situations where clients do not pay their bills (for any number of reasons)

    d. The need to establish awareness of the new company very rapidly in the industry so that you will get a chance to bid on new projects

    e. The need to offer a pricing structure lower than that of the major companies currently operating in the business, in order to interest prospective companies in trying the services of your organization.

Each of the above options, plus a great many more, can have a significant impact on the way your consulting business is positioned and the methods that you will use to prospect for new clients.

3. *A definition of the consulting practice.* This section of the plan will provide a description of what services the consulting organization does and does not offer. For example, if you were a personnel consultant with special expertise in employee incentive programs, you would develop a definition of your practice that would describe the nature of your work in this area. The definition might be as follows:

> The JAG Consulting business seeks to build a large practice serving the profit sector by providing incentive programs for employees that will increase their productivity and their overall commitment to their jobs.
> The objective of the marketing program for this practice is to develop a national reputation for providing the most effective employee incentive programs. Our efforts will focus on securing consulting engagements with selling organizations; however, the practice will also have the capability to develop effective programs for employee groups involved with customer service.
> The consulting practice will not work on other personnel-related projects such as compensation, organizational structure, employee relations, or benefits, in order to maintain a very specific focus in the services that are offered to prospective clients.

4. *Structure of the business.* This section of the plan should outline how the business will be organized, considering such things as the following:

    a. The number of employees by function

    b. The types/qualifications of the people who fill the top positions in the company

    c. The reporting relationships

    d. The role of outside services in the operations of the business. For example, this would identify those functional areas of the practice that will be subcontracted to others and what the present thinking is regarding efforts to bring these functions in house

    e. The longer-term plans for the structure of your practice. For example, your plan may call for only two people at first, but the plan provides for the addition of two more in year one, three in year two, and three more in year three

5. *Business plan strategies.* This section of the plan should contain brief statements—normally one page or less—of the strategic philosophy of the organization regarding a few key areas, such as

    a. Overall company positioning

    b. Target audience definition

    c. Communications strategy

    d. Sales strategy

    e. Customer service strategy

    f. Pricing/fee strategy

6. *Company operating plans.* Many organizations consider this section to be the most important part of the plan, as it is where the business outlines the programs it anticipates implementing in order to carry out the strategies developed in the previous section. It is in this section that you should outline your plans for the year regarding:

    a. Building awareness of the organization among the target audience. This includes such things as advertising efforts, speaking engagements, publishing plans, or any similar activities that will get the name of your practice in front of prospective clients.

    b. Generating leads for the practice that can be developed into new business. This would include a discussion of specific programs that you may implement to motivate prospective clients to call you and might contain plans for direct mail programs, involvement in specific industry groups, cold-call contacts, and the like.

c. Designing company brochures, selling materials, leave-behind promotional pieces, and so on.

d. Developing the specific program that will be implemented to sell your services to prospective clients. Will you be the primary sales person, or will you rely on others to sell for you? Will you sell based on leads only, or will you try to sell on a cold-call basis? You should also identify the sales aids that you will develop to make your selling more effective, such things as examples of your work, development of video tapes, and other materials.

e. Defining the plan that the company will implement to ensure that it will service its clientele effectively. For example, will you work at the clients' premises or at your offices? What actions will you take in regular contact with your clients, so that each feels that their business is important to you and you are committed to providing them with a high level of service? You might mention in this section your commitment to having a car phone, providing clients with your home telephone number, assigning people in your company the specific responsibility of keeping in contact with some clients on a regular basis, and similar measures, etc.

7. *Financial plans and projections.* For many businesses, this section of the plan represents the extent of the planning that is done each year. However, it really should simply be a section of the overall plan. It should contain the following elements:

a. A revenue projection for the company for the next one to three years

b. A pro forma P&L for the business for the plan year

c. A source-of-business analysis

d. A cash flow projection for the year

e. An overview of the fee structure, accompanied by a rationale indicating how the levels have been established

8. *Assumptions, risks, and concerns.* This section should identify the key assumptions upon which the plan was based, to the extent necessary for a noninvolved reader to understand the plan.

This section also should identify what you believe to be the risks and concerns relative to your business that might impact most on your ability to meet the objectives in your business plan. It might consider such things as the following:

a. Competitive reactions to the entrance of your consulting organization into the market

b. Possible government legislation that could impact on the principal areas of consulting in which you are operating or the way you plan to consult to clients

c. Potential problems with your former employer as a result of your departure to start your own company

d. Unforseen difficulties in hiring employees for specific positions within the company

9. *Appendices.* In addition to the main sections, your business plan should include a series of appendices providing additional information germane to the overall operation of your business. While the content of the appendices depends upon the consulting practice, the following are some of the most common topics covered in this section of the plan.

a. *Job descriptions.* This would contain written job descriptions for the key operating people in your company, including for each position such things as the upward and downward reporting relationships associated with the position; the overall job objective (i.e., what will be the main priority of the person); the job responsibilities (i.e., what is the individual charged with doing on a day-to-day basis to achieve the established objectives); and job qualifications (in terms of what skills are required to fill the position).

b. *Detailed financial statements.* This would include estimates (i.e., projections) of the expenses that you will incur in the coming months, broken out by very detailed cost categories. This is the source document on which the basic financial statement of the organization will be based.

c. *External support and advisory services.* Some consulting businesses are very dependent on subcontractors. Often, the identification of these subcontractors can be a very important credibility builder for the organization, particularly if it is a new company seeking to establish itself with the financial community. Therefore, a brief discussion of your key subcontractors may be essential to a thorough overall plan.

SUMMARY

Now that you have completed this chapter on the overall structure of the business plan, you are ready to begin to develop each of the elements that will go into the actual plan. It would be very easy to read this material and say that you have thought through all the issues and know what is needed and therefore need not write it down in a formal document. If you take this posture, read no further, as the balance of this book will be of very limited value to you. The effective planning and marketing of a consulting practice requires a commitment to thought *and* writing. I feel strongly that you will do your best thinking if you are forced to commit it to writing. The first step in this process involves the definition of the business in which you are operating and the client base you will serve.

4 Defining the Business

This chapter is intended to help you define your consulting practice from two basic perspectives. First, we will discuss the importance of being able to define the nature of your services in such a way that the business will have clear direction and scope, as well as vision for the future. Then we will discuss the target audience for your consulting practice, in terms of developing a definition of this prospective client and then identifying the specific individuals and organizations that meet the criteria you have established.

You might be wondering why it is important, or even necessary, to go through the process of defining your practice, since you will take whatever projects you can get, just to generate some revenues. This "take what you can get" attitude is very common among new entrepreneurs in the consulting business, but it is a very short-term strategy for building a practice. If you develop a strategy relative to what you want to be and, importantly, what you are not, the chances of achieving your objectives for the practice are dramatically greater than if you pursue a strategy of accepting any work you can get.

KNOWING WHAT BUSINESS YOU ARE IN

There are many examples of organizations that have failed because they never understood the business they really were in and, therefore, were unable to advance with the trends in their industry. Consultants who do not keep up with the times and well ahead of their clients will quickly lose their ability to be of effective use. Consider the following case histories of two different product-oriented industries and one consulting practice that had difficulty defining what they were and thus were not prepared for the future resulting in their virtual demise.

Buggy whips. In the late 1880s, several thriving organizations produced buggy whips, essential equipment for most Americans if they were to get appropriate locomotion from the horses pulling their carriages. Unfortunately, the organizations that manufactured buggy whips thought of themselves only in terms of the precise end product they delivered to customers. Yet the demand for buggy whips declined significantly when the automobile became popular in the early 1900s. At the same time, people using the new automobiles were more in need of goggles, gloves, blankets, and scarves. Over time, as the buggy whip industry virtually disappeared, companies that manufactured accessory products for the automobile grew at very accelerated rates. The key was that the buggy whip manufacturers did not understand that they really were in the business of transportation accessories; had they realized this, they might have looked to the future and become the companies that developed and marketed the many accessory products for the automobile.

Matches. During the first half of the twentieth century, cigarette smoking was very common among Americans, with well over 50 percent of all adults smoking in the 1950s. A necessary item to light up a cigarette (or cigar or pipe) was either a match or a lighter, and there were major differences between these two product types: Matches were cheap (or free) and disposable and often carried an advertising message; lighters, on the other hand, were relatively expensive and, therefore, nondisposable and did not carry advertising messages. During these years, the companies that produced matches viewed the lighter manufacturers as their competition, reasoning that the more consumers purchased (and used) lighters, the fewer matches they would use.

The more lighters-fewer matches scenario was correct, as consumption was finite. However, the approach was not right for the situation. The book-match companies were more likely to face competition from the manufacturers of other secondary advertising vehicles, such as key chains, pens, or letter openers. If the match companies had thought of themselves as providing a unique source of advertising rather than simply a product for lighting cigarettes, the twelve major manufacturers that were in this business in the 1950s might all still be around today, instead of the six that managed to survive in the very small industry that remains. Conceivably they even might have been the ones to develop the other specialty advertising vehicles that are used today, such as supermarket carts, in-store video, transit advertising and the like.

The coupon consultancy.　Throughout the 1960s, 1970s, and 1980s, consumer coupons were a major part of the promotional program of many different companies that distributed their products through supermarkets. Many companies spent more money on couponing than they did on advertising. In this era, consulting organizations were established for the purpose of working with companies to make their coupon programs more effective through selecting the correct media in which to distribute coupons, the most effective values in light of client objectives, and the correct approach to budgeting for these efforts.

Although coupon use continues to grow each year and more and more coupons are distributed, the demand for specialists in couponing has declined. Client organizations have gained considerable experience with coupons and no longer need to pay large sums of money to have consultants advise them on the most appropriate use of the device. As a result, many people who were in this business have found their practices faltering, requiring them to make major adjustments in their approaches to consulting. Some have left the field, others have found work in the coupon programs of client organizations. Still others have recognized that they defined their business poorly (or not at all) and have made major adjustments to survive.

If these consultants had originally defined their practices as being in the promotional consulting business, rather than the coupon consulting business, they all might have been able to survive and probably thrive. They would have focused their attention on all types of consumer promotions—contests, sweepstakes, premium offers, refunds, and so on—seeking to advise clients on the best way to achieve their overall marketing/promotional objectives via the use of all types of promotion rather than simply the application of couponing.

At the present time, there are many people who feel that the promotional consulting companies need to consider redefining their business to include a broader perspective, since promotion is in competition with advertising and public relations for available marketing funds. The futurists who study marketing consulting suggest that the organization of the future will be the one that can provide consulting services in promotion, advertising and public relations and will need to focus more on the total communication with the consumer, rather than on the use of any one vehicle to accomplish this task.

In summary, you need to ask yourself constantly whether you are thinking broadly enough about your consulting practice to enable you to grow with the trends in your industry. Or are you finding yourself in the same position as the buggy whip manufacturer? All it takes is some in-depth thought and analysis about your business.

Defining Your Consulting Practice

In defining the nature of your consulting practice, a few very basic issues that relate to almost all types of consulting should be considered. If you think analytically about each of these, you will have a significantly greater probability of developing a definition for your business that will dramatically increase its chances of longevity.

1. *What type of clientele is your consulting practice dedicated to serving, and are they likely to be around essentially the same format 10 to 15 years from now?* If the nature of the client universe is likely to undergo major changes, then you can be certain that the types of services that clients will require from outside consultants will change as well.

2. *Does your business really offer any unique expertise that clients could not get from their own people if they had sufficient manpower?* Some clients use consultants primarily as extra hands so that they can avoid adding permanent staff when funds are tight. If your consulting practice is like this, you must be very alert to the way your clients' needs change regarding outside services, since your products must change in direct reaction to your clients' requirements.

3. *Can you describe your business very quickly and easily to a person who is completely uninvolved with the industry?* This is perhaps the single most important consideration in defining a

business. If you have thought through what business you are really in, you should be able to tell someone about it in a very brief period of time without the need for any audiovisual aids. To illustrate this, I frequently use the example of the elevator ride in my teaching: Suppose you're going into a fifteen-story office building to make a new business presentation to the senior vice president of the functional area responsible for purchasing your services. While you are waiting for the elevator, the president of the company arrives. Fortunately, you had been introduced to him before in a social situation, so he recognizes you when he approaches. As he comes toward the elevator, he acknowledges you and asks why you are there. You reply, "To make a new business call on Ms. Doe," at which moment the elevator door opens, and you both step inside. The button for 10 is pushed and the president asks, "What business are you in these days?" You now have 10 floors to describe your business in a very meaningful way to a person who could have the greatest influence over whether you get the assignment. If you describe your business in an easy-to-understand and convincing manner, the outlook could be bright; if you don't, you could leave the impression that you are confused about what you do and, therefore, probably would not be able to keep the prospective client.

4. *Can you describe the following two scenarios:*

- The ideal consulting assignment, in terms of such factors as the nature of the work that would be requested, the type of company that would be seeking your services, the size of the assignment relative to annual revenues (or projects), and the geographical area that would be involved.

- The types of consulting assignments that you are capable of completing effectively. This should include a definition of the task to be performed, the revenue levels available, the type of company seeking the service, the timing required to complete the work, and so on.

If you are able to describe the above two examples well, then you are likely to complete the process of defining your business very effectively.

An example of a well-defined consulting practice. In my consulting practice, we operate a specialized service to client organizations, which I will use as an example of an effective way to define a practice. The business that will be described involves providing qualitative research services to clients. Qualitative research is market research that focuses on providing diagnostic inputs based on in-depth discussions with relatively small numbers of people, as opposed to quantitative research, which develops numerically based information as a result of interviews with large numbers of respondents. The most common form of qualitative research is focus groups; this is the particular specialty that we feature to our clients. Focus groups consist of structured discussions with approximately ten persons selected for common characteristics (these could be product usage similarities, common ages, radio listening patterns, etc.). They are led by a trained moderator through a discussion of a topic, for the purpose of acquiring as much in-depth information as possible about the feelings of the group toward the subject at hand. This research technique has become the most widely used of any form of market research in the United States today, and the methodology is expected to be very broadly used for many years to come.

We describe our qualitative research/focus groups business as follows:

1. *General description.* Broadly, we provide qualitative research services to client organizations. The principal service we offer is focus group research; however, other forms of qualitative research are also available if they are more appropriate for the client, relative to the objectives of the project being considered.

2. *Description of the clientele.* This practice seeks to serve any clients in product or service areas where a high level of technical product knowledge is not required to understand the problem being explored. Further, the target clientele ideally will be large companies with significant research budgets, preferably (though not essentially) located east of the Mississippi River (to minimize travel).

3. *Unique expertise.* The unique expertise we bring to this business consists of the following specific elements:
   a. The individuals who conduct the focus groups are strategic marketing consultants first and moderators second and, therefore, bring to the table a more strategic and general marketing

perspective than is available from the traditional focus group moderator.

   b. The people who conduct the groups are highly trained and experienced people who have had a minimum of ten years experience in marketing, research, or consulting. This is a strong point of difference between the service we offer and that of most competitors.

   c. We have established a national reputation for our work in this area, by virtue of our prior assignments with satisfied clients and because of the book I published on the subject (*The Practical Handbook and Guide to Focus Group Research*) in late 1987.

   d. Finally, we have developed some techniques for moderating groups that are unique to our organization and that we believe enable our clients to get more out of the sessions we conduct than is possible with standard focus group methods.

4. *Quick definition of the business.* When asked, we define our work as representing a "unique approach to focus group research," manifested by the experience of our people, the strategic thrust of our work in this area, and the innovative methods we have developed for conducting groups. On occasion, we also must define a focus group as part of this quick definition, and we are prepared to do that for the few clients who require this information. We hope that the message communicated by our quick definition accomplishes two key objectives:

   a. It communicates that we are professionals in this area and that we have some very unique things to offer clients who retain our organization to conduct their focus groups.

   b. It leads to further questions relative to a description of the specific techniques that make us different and the backgrounds of the people who conduct the focus groups.

When Is It Time to Redefine the Business?

Many managers of small consulting businesses worry about becoming too specialized and therefore missing out on the hot new trends that might dramatically increase the size of their practice. Normally, however, the answer to the question of whether to redefine the business is *don't*, unless it is absolutely necessary. The old saying "if it ain't broke, don't fix it" is very appropriate in this situation. If business is good and trends are continuing in a positive direction, then there is usually no reason to consider redefining the business. On the other hand, if there are some questions about the state of the business at the current time, redefining the nature of the practice might be advisable. There are a few key signs that you might look for as a preliminary indication:

1. Are revenues declining? Are revenues coming from different types of client organizations? Are fewer clients accounting for the bulk of the revenues compared to previous years?

2. Has the absolute number of clients declined? Is the practice getting new clients in the same numbers as in previous years? Is the nature of the client universe changing in terms of the size, location, or type of company that is seeking the services?

3. Over the past few years, have any significant structural or technological changes surfaced in the industry or industries that your consulting business serves? (This type of situation can create significant opportunities for a consulting business that is already very well connected to an industry and can be the type of environmental change that might call for a redefinition of the business.)

Summary

If you go through this type of exercise for your consulting service, the definition that ultimately results should be a much more powerful tool in helping to generate new clients than it would have been had you not gone through this effort. One cannot place too much emphasis on the development of an effective definition of the consulting practice. It is important both in describing (to prospective clients, suppliers, or possible employees) what the practice does and in determining what it does not do.

DEFINING THE TARGET AUDIENCE

One of the keys to a successful consulting business is identifying the right people to whom to sell your services. You could have the best consulting product available, but if you do not direct your marketing and sales effort at the people who are potential buyers, then your efforts may well be wasted.

A person starting a small consulting company may feel that some of the ideas in this section simply are not for him or her. Why should a one-person company that is simply seeking to generate clients for a new venture go through all the trouble of formalizing the development of the target audience? In my opinion, this exercise is at least as important for a small start-up venture as it is for a company with an existing client base and an ongoing source of referrals. Indeed, the more established company is less likely to need a formal target audience definition than the newer, smaller one, because so many of its prospects come over the transom as opposed to being identified as a result of an outreach effort.

There are a few significant reasons why it is in the best interests of a new company (or an existing one) to take the time necessary to determine who the target audience should be. The exercise forces you to think through your business in order to determine what types of customers are most likely to purchase your services. This self-analysis is, in and of itself, a very valuable thing to do, as it increases the chances that the services you offer will be appropriate for the audience to whom they are directed. Moreover, the definition provides a target toward which you can direct your marketing and sales activities. If you do not define a target audience, your people may not know whom to call on for new business, whom to direct mailings or advertising to—on whom they should focus their efforts. Thus, defining a target audience increases the efficiency and effectiveness of the marketing and sales activities of a consulting organization. Specifically, mailings, advertising or promotion efforts, or sales calls can be directed at a much smaller and more defined group of organizations, which will result in considerable savings. Finally, the exercise will help you determine with whom you do *not* want to do business. Not all prospects will be appropriate for your organization, because of their industry, their size, their needs, and so on. By establishing a well-defined description of the target customer, you will be able to evaluate inquiries from prospective clients to determine whether they are worth following up for future business development.

How To Develop a Target Audience Definition

The target audience is defined as the people who are most likely to purchase your consulting product or service. This definition should be described as precisely as possible to assist you in directing your marketing and sales activities more effectively. The definition of a target audience for a consulting business should have several different elements. For example, often it is necessary to include an industry descriptor, (transportation business, radio or television, financial services, etc.). This begins to focus your targeting efforts, as it certainly is easier to direct a marketing and sales program at one industry than at the entire universe of businesses. Secondly, a target audience definition normally contains a functional identifier, (i.e., corporate treasury, marketing research department, etc.) which establishes who in an organization is most likely to purchase your product or service. Finally, a well-thought-out target audience definition often also includes some information about the size or geographic location of the organizations to whom your company will be directing efforts. For example, the distance of a target company from your home base may limit your interest in providing service. Do you want the focus of your practice to be worldwide, national, or regional in scope? The degree to which this is identified will be very helpful in marketing to a target audience.

The size of the corporation (or organization) you are appealing to also could be very important. Some consultants only want to work with the very largest companies, whereas others want to target only very small ones. This is an individual decision that will depend on the objectives of your consulting business and the nature of the practice. In addition, some consultants will only work for the leading companies in a particular industry, as they want their image to be associated with high-quality, well-respected clients. For instance, some consultants in the communications industry will only work for a radio or TV station that is one of the three leaders in the market, whereas others will work for any station in the market. Do what works best for you but focus your efforts in a specific direction. Make a conscious decision to act based on the opportunity that you have identified.

The process of defining a target audience should be very similar for every organization, regardless of the type of consulting business that is being formed. If you follow the steps identified in this chapter, you will end up with an effective definition of your target audience that should serve you well for a long time.

Step #1. Determine your own company objectives in relation to the potential definition of the target audience. Do you intend to become a specialist within a particular industry or will you offer your service to a variety of different industries? This is a very important decision for the overall marketing and positioning of your practice; therefore, it must be made only after considerable analysis of the opportunities. Many consultants find it best to focus their activities within one industry; others find that one of their biggest assets is that they work in a variety of different industries.

Industry specialization allows you to become an expert in your specific field, establishing a reputation based on this experience. It also enables you to leverage your own time very effectively—if you work in one specific business, you do not have a lot of time to learn about a business that is new to you. Moreover, industry specialization facilitates new business efforts, since you can focus your activities much more specifically as a result of attendance at industry meetings, speeches you give, articles written, and so on. Finally, specializing in one area makes it much easier to stay up-to-date about new trends and developments in the industry, since you only have to stay abreast of one field.

The disadvantages of specialization involve several different considerations. First, some industries are structured in such a way that consulting organizations cannot concentrate on them without creating confidentiality problems with clients. For example, in an industry with only five to ten competitors, it might be impossible for a consultant to work for more than one company at a time or to finish with one client and go on to another before waiting a considerable amount of time. However, there are some industries, such as radio or television stations, banks, insurance companies, retailing or automotive dealers, where one could specialize within the field and avoid competitive conflicts between organizations, primarily because of the geographical boundary limitations of the marketing and sales efforts in these categories.

Second, with specialization, you put all your eggs in one basket. If you work in only one industry and the industry comes on very hard times, the impact on your practice potentially could be devastating.

Third, many consultants do not concentrate on a single industry because they feel that they will provide a better end product to their clients if they can draw from their experiences in other industries to solve problems. In my consulting career, certainly, I have found this to be a very valuable benefit; we frequently have solved problems in one industry based on our experiences in another.

An absolutely essential part of the process of the target audience definition is deciding what types of consulting services you will provide, even though this relates primarily to the nature of your consulting practice. Hopefully, you will have already made this decision (based on the material presented earlier in this chapter) before you even start your consulting practice; if not, now is the time to do so. In essence, you must define as precisely as possible the product/service that you will offer to your clients. You should be able to list on a single sheet of paper, using very brief phrases, all the services that your organization will offer to its clients.

In the development of individual objectives for a target audience, you need to determine how the type of service you provide fits into the needs of different-size companies. For example, if you offer a consulting service that specializes in the stock transfer business, you can generally assume that the target audience will be relatively large public companies. On the other hand, if you are offering assistance in advertising copy development or media planning, you might find that the best clients are smaller organizations that do not have these capabilities in house. Further, if the people in your company are more comfortable working with smaller companies, where access to the decision maker is much easier and the corporate bureaucracy is less cumbersome, this, too, should be included among your objectives.

Finally, some consulting organizations have very specific guidelines regarding how far they are willing to travel to service clients; others view the world as their marketplace—to them, distance is not important, as long as they can provide service that is consistent with their overall quality and at a fee that is acceptable.

Step #2. Identify the types of organizations that use the types of services that your consultancy will offer. In the classes I have taught over the years, I have found that some people find this to be the most difficult part of the process of developing a target audience definition. Frequently, students will ask how they can possibly know what types of companies could use their services. Typically, my response to such inquiries is that if prospective consultants do not have a reasonable idea of the broad scope of the target audience for their product, they probably are not ready to begin their own businesses. You should be familiar with the types of organizations that currently use (or could potentially benefit from) the type of service you will offer; if you aren't, it is unlikely that you have had enough experience in the field to function as a consultant.

For the purpose of this discussion, we will assume that you have a general sense of your target audience and you now need to prioritize the potential target audience according to the prospective organizations that are most desirable. You should begin the process of refining the target audience definition by listing all the industries that qualify as a potential target audience segment (this is particularly appropriate for consulting organizations that have decided to focus on industry specialization in one or more areas). Then develop a list of the major companies in each of the industries that qualify. Later in this chapter, we will provide some suggestions as to how to develop such a list.

If your approach is more functional (e.g., personnel departments, market research departments), your task is more difficult. Unfortunately, there is no simple and easy way to determine the types of companies (by industry, size, structure, etc.) that might use the services that you will offer. I recommend that you undertake at least some of the following activities to assist you in this identification process:

- Talk with key people in relevant industry trade associations, as they are normally very familiar with what is happening in the member organizations. These trade associations could be industry specific (i.e., radio advertising, bank marketing association, soap and detergent) or more targeted to functional areas within an industry (i.e., compensation, personnel, marketing, etc.). If you talk to people in these organizations about the services they provide, you are likely to get excellent help, generally at no cost. Further, you might make some good contacts that could become referral sources in the future.

- Talk with people in tangential businesses and ask for their inputs regarding potential target clients for your business. If these organizations do not view you as competition, they might be very helpful in identifying target customers, based on their experiences with different kinds of organizations. As with trade associations, these discussions could also have value well beyond the immediate information you garner, as they, too, could lead to the establishment of good contacts.

- Read a large number of business publications for industries that appear to be of interest to you or in functional areas close to your specialty. These publications tend to provide excellent insight. You also would find it very helpful to meet with the editors of the most relevant publications to obtain their suggestions about appropriate targets for your consulting services.

- Conduct some marketing research to help define your target audience. This research could be very informal, consisting simply of telephone calls to several different organizations to determine whom you should talk with about your particular area of specialty, followed by calls to these individuals to set up appointments for your business presentation. This process will be very instructive to you in terms of defining the types of organizations that purchase the services you offer and discovering which are likely to be realistic target candidates. Another option is formal research, where you hire an outside research company to conduct a brief survey of a variety of companies in different industries, in order to determine what types of organizations purchase the services you offer. This alternative clearly provides the most meaningful help on target audience definition; however, it is also the most expensive approach.

Step #3. Determine the decision-making function in the target customers and identify the specific people that should be contacted. This is a very important part of the process of identifying the target audience for your service, because you can offer a terrific service, call on the correct organization, and still not succeed because you made the sales presentation to the wrong person. A great many people in American industry have the ability/authority to say "no" when it comes to a purchasing decision, but relatively few have the authority to say "yes." This is particularly true for consulting services, as hiring a consultant frequently requires a higher level of approval authority than do other purchases of similar dollar value.

Identifying the decision maker who can purchase the services you provide is probably the most difficult part of the entire target audience definition process. Larger companies will have a different approval authority than do smaller ones, and some industries decentralize decision making more than others. Consequently, to define the target audience down to the particular person in question, it is necessary to contact the target companies and ask who is responsible for decisions regarding the function you offer. Once you identify this individual, it still may be difficult to arrange a meeting, since these people often have subordinates who screen service organizations of all types (the "no" people) before they agree to meet with representatives.

How to Identify Specific Target Customers

A large number of different resources are available to assist you in identifying specific companies that might be appropriate targets for your products or services. The following list describes some of the more popular sources. However, this is only intended to give you a start; you should consult the reference librarian at a public library in a major city for information as to other sources that might be helpful.

1. *Membership lists of trade associations.* Most trade associations will provide, either free or for a small charge, a list of their membership. The thoroughness of the lists and the amount of information they provide will vary significantly by organization. However, if you have identified a specific industry as a good potential target for your business, this list should be a very useful resource.

2. *List of participants in trade association meetings or conventions.* Another excellent source of leads regarding possible prospects for your consulting service would be a list of the organizations/people that attend trade association meetings dealing with your area of expertise. A list of the participants of a well-targeted trade association meeting could also provide two other very important pieces of information. First, by evaluating the types of organizations/functions of the people who attend, you could probably improve your ability to identify other possible target organizations simply by developing a description of the typical attendee and then applying that to the universe at large to find other organizations that meet these criteria. Second, trade meetings are common gathering places for consultants. Frequently, the attendee list will describe the type of business of each of the attendees, so you will gain some sense of the competition you will face when you seek to sell your services to this class of trade.

3. *Industry publications.* A third excellent source of leads would be trade magazines targeted to the specific industry or function in which you have an interest. See what companies advertise, who

subscribes (often the publication will sell a list of subscribers), and who writes or is written about in the publications. A great number of industry trade magazines also publish an annual buying guide that lists all the companies in the industry, what they buy, and who are the key contacts. Some publications even provide basic information about each company (as it relates to the buying requirements of the industry publications), which you may find valuable when you are evaluating the potential of an organization as a prospective client.

4. *The Advertiser Redbook.* This book is published by National Register Publishing Company and is available in most large city public libraries. It provides information about most companies in the United States that spend any meaningful monies on advertising in either consumer or trade publications. This book can be particularly helpful, as it provides a considerable amount of information about these companies, such as names and titles of key executives, company size and number of employees, subsidiary divisions, and the nature of the business.

5. *Thomas' Register.* The Thomas' Register is an excellent source of company names and addresses, indexed by industry. With this document, it is possible to identify a few industries that represent excellent potential for possible consulting assignments and then target a mailing to specific companies based on the descriptive information provided in the guide.

6. *Specialized directories.* A large number of special directories provide very useful information about prospective companies. For example, Monitor Publishing Company in New York City sells several different guides that give excellent information about prospective clients. Some examples of these are *The Financial 1000,* a directory of the people who manage the 1000 leading U.S. financial organizations, *The Over The Counter 1000,* a directory of the people who manage the 1000 younger growth companies in the United States, and *The Corporate 1000,* a directory of the people who manage the leading 1000 U.S. companies. Monitor also publishes guides about Canadian business, international companies, and several different editions about the government. And this is only one of several organizations that publish lists of

companies that could be very helpful in developing effective target audience groups.

SUMMARY

Defining the target audience for your consulting business is a key part of the planning process, and, if done well, it can have a significant impact on the overall effectiveness of the marketing and sales program that you implement. Remember, though, that you should be as precise as possible without being too limiting—you don't want to define a target group that is so specific that it does not have enough people in it to provide the basis for a meaningful business. To this end, it is vital to take the time to try to quantify the universe of the target audience in terms of the number of potential contacts that exist.

5 Developing a Company Identity

The company identity is how others see the organization, what the business is called; it is a strong statement of what the company is and what it stands for. In essence, the company identity is the personality of the organization, its way of dressing, and even its overall mood and attitude.

Several different important elements go into the establishment of a company identity. Briefly, they may be stated as follows:

- The communications message that the company uses to say what it is and what the organization stands for in its area of practice

- The graphic look that the company chooses for all external communications

- The office environment—both the decor of the office and the tone in which business is conducted

- The name of the company

THE COMPANY POSITIONING

Before any of these elements can be finalized, however, you must develop a company positioning. *Positioning* has been a very important

47

buzzword in the advertising and marketing community since the early 1970s, when the advertising agency Trout & Reis coined the term in a series of three articles for *Advertising Age* in 1972. The concept behind positioning is that you decide what you want people (presumably, your target customers and prospects) to think about your company when they hear its name, and then you develop communications vehicles that help to achieve that objective. The key to the positioning concept is that *you are seeking to reserve a place for your identity in the consumer's mind and that image or "position" should be unique to you.* In effect, you try to own an idea or an image that is consistent with the overall message you wish to communicate to the target audience. Some examples of well-known positionings might help to demonstrate this point.

The name Marlboro inevitably conjures up an image of a cowboy riding the range. This very western, macho image is what the company wants consumers to think about when they see the Marlboro brand or hear the Marlboro name. By establishing a positioning using the cowboy, Marlboro sends a message to target consumers that, if they want to be associated with the image that the cowboy conveys, Marlboro may very well be the brand for them.

When you think of a BMW automobile, you probably have a very different mental image of the person driving the car than you do when you think of Chevrolet, Nissan, or Cadillac. BMW has worked very hard to develop a positioning for itself as "the ultimate driving machine" and as a car that appeals to the yuppie set in America. The image is very different from that of other expensive foreign (or domestic) cars and this is deliberate—it is with this difference that the people at BMW hope to appeal strongly to their target market.

My final example of positioning relates to a service, as opposed to a product. American Express has used its more stringent qualification requirements to establish an image based on snob appeal. The message is that the American Express card is different from bank cards like Visa or MasterCard—it is the card for people who have made it or at least are on the way.

Within the consulting business, it is often more difficult to identify a positioning that is unique to the practice and meaningful to the prospective client base, because the consulting product is much less tangible than cars, cards, or cigarettes. Therefore, when planning a positioning for a consulting organization, it is necessary to think through very carefully what the practice is to stand for, selecting a simple-to-communicate distillation of this message. In most cases, the positioning for a consulting practice should be stated in very few words that effectively identify the place the organization has in the market. The positioning definition of our focus group business discussed in Chapter 4 was "a unique approach to focus group research." This brief statement is intended to create a different and potent identity for the research services that we offer to clients, to set us apart from others who feel that they offer comparable services in the industry.

Why Establish a Position?

My students frequently ask me, why establish a position? This question is especially common among those people who are operating (or are planning to establish) a one-person consulting organization. For them, the focus is generally on just getting some clients so they can begin to reap benefits from the practice. They often comment that their company will not do any advertising, so why should they go through the exercise of developing a positioning. Further, some of them argue that they really are not any different from the other people who operate in their segment of the consulting business and therefore they have difficulty saying something about their practice in a positioning statement that would be meaningful to prospective clients. To these last, I always say that, *if a consultant feels that he or she is just like everyone else in the industry (or functional area) in which he or she competes or is about to enter, then he or she should think very seriously about going into the consulting business at all.* One of the most basic tenets of marketing is to provide the prospective customer with a reason why—a reason for using your organization instead of another. If you cannot articulate some meaningful reason why a client should retain your organization, there may not be a place for your practice as you currently conceive it. At the very least, you need to go back to the drawing board and figure out what you can say about your consulting service that would be meaningful to prospective customers.

I believe there are a few very important reasons why every consulting service needs to establish a position. First, a clearly articulated position provides a focus for all the communications that will emerge from the consulting practice: the look and feel of the business card, the content of the company brochure, and the graphic approach to all external advertising and public relations activities. In essence, the positioning ensures that all communications are consistent with the chosen message (both verbal and nonverbal). A positioning also provides a structure for the activities that the organization undertakes to attract new business and clients. The methods used to find new business should be very dependent on the position that the organization has developed. A consulting organization that wishes to be viewed a high-quality/high-priced entry into the business would develop a very different type of brochure than would an organization that wishes to position itself as a consultant for even the smallest organization.

Finally, the need to establish a position for the organization represents a valuable discipline, forcing you to think through what your company really offers prospective clients. Because of the intangible nature of consulting, it is vital for the people who own and operate the business to develop a reason why for their company that will be meaningful to prospective clients. If one does not work through the development of a positioning, this type of thinking probably will never occur.

How to Establish a Positioning

Although a certain amount of mystique surrounds the notion of positioning development, in reality, there is a very systematic process that you can undertake to develop a positioning for your organization. This process involves nine steps.

Step #1. Determine the overall focus of your consulting practice. Make decisions regarding such issues as whether your consulting practice will focus its efforts on a specific industry in a particular discipline or establish a reputation as an expert in a functional area and offer that service to a large number of industries. Regardless of what you decide, your choice will represent a very important strategic business decision that will have significant implications on the ultimate positioning that will be established for your practice. Some examples will illustrate the range of possibilities.

- A compensation consulting company might decide to focus its practice on the communications industry, seeking to sell its expertise exclusively to radio and television stations, newspapers, and magazines. This approach to a business focus is very popular, as it allows the organization to become an authority in an industry, generating extensive credibility in its area of expertise.

- A sales training consulting company might decide to focus its efforts on retail business, training store personnel in the techniques of effective retail sales.

- A marketing research consulting company might decide to offer qualitative research to any industry. Similar to the other examples, this organization has identified a functional area of specialty but has chosen to be somewhat less focused in its approach to sourcing business.

Step #2. Identify the strengths and weaknesses of your organization. Develop a list of the strengths and weaknesses inherent in your organization. Be as detailed as possible and try to work from the perspective of a client looking at the practice. Consider such areas as quality of service, pricing/value, experience of the principals, breadth of product line offering, ability to provide fast turnaround, analytical skills, technical expertise, manpower levels, and geographical location vis-à-vis the client universe. The key is to provide an honest and thorough articulation of the practice's primary strong and weak points, both in absolute terms and relative to the competition.

Step #3. Evaluate the competition. Assess the most significant strengths and weaknesses of the major competitive consulting companies. The areas to be covered are essentially the same areas as those listed in Step #2. Perform the assessment of the competitive strengths and weaknesses from the perspective of what is important to your prospective customer universe, as regards their needs for consulting assistance. An important part of this evaluation is to determine the positioning of the key competitive companies, as communicated in their brochures, presentations, or advertising.

Step #4. Develop a "positioning pie" for your area of consulting. A positioning pie will simplify the analysis of your competitors' communications stories. Identifying the positioning approaches of the major factors in the industry and then grouping your various competitors into their appropriate wedges will provide insight into the positioning alternatives available to your organization. Have some strategic approaches been employed by many different consulting firms, making them unlikely candidates for your company? Conversely, are there any positioning approaches that the competition has not adopted, which might be open to an entry by your organization? This could be indicated by a blank wedge in the pie or one where several organizations exist, but none has developed a dominant—or even meaningful—position from what you judge to be the perspective of the prospective client organization.

Developing a positioning pie is a three-step process. First, determine the various strategic alternatives that a consulting organization might adopt. This requires an analysis of the various options that already exist in the industry, as well as some brainstorming on your part. Next, label the perimeter of a circle with each of the strategic approaches that you have identified. The size of each piece of pie should correspond to the relative size of the consulting segment that is represented by the strategic designation on the perimeter of the pie. Finally, assign each of the major competitors to the piece of the pie that is closest to the positioning that the organization is using. Normally, several companies will fall into a variety of different categories, and some categories will be empty.

Figure 5.1 is an example of a positioning pie for a marketing consulting company that is seeking to develop a positioning based on the services that it provides to the radio industry. In this case, the consulting organization has decided that it wishes to specialize in radio, both because of the unique knowledge of programming of its personnel and because it considers that specialization in this industry will yield large profits. If the pie in the figure is a reasonably accurate representation of the consulting marketplace in the radio industry, the areas of audience promotion and advertising and positioning may be an appropriate niche for this company, because both categories appear to be reasonably large, but neither has significant numbers of companies competing for the business. If the company implementing this analysis has expertise in these areas, then it certainly should consider them for its consulting positioning.

Step #5. Identify the primary hiring criteria of prospective clients. Develop a list identifying in order of importance, the various factors that influence prospective clients' selection of consulting organizations. A key criterion for an effective company positioning is the communication of

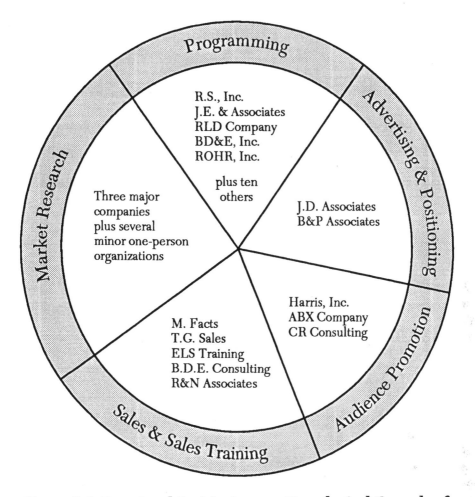

Figure 5.1 Functional Positionings—a Hypothetical Example of the Marketing Pie

a service that ties closely with an established need within the client universe.

Step #6. Develop a matrix of the market's needs and your organization's strengths. Make a simple graph to determine the point where your strengths and your target customers' needs intersect. List consumer needs on one axis and your consulting group's strengths on the other, then draw lines extending across the graph from each point on the axes. Wherever an important consumer demand and an optimum company strength intersect represents a potential positioning area for your consulting organization.

Step #7. Match the key points on the matrix with the information contained in the positioning pie. As soon as you have completed your two graphs, compare them to determine which positioning alternatives are not only suitable but available (or possible) to adopt. This is a very important part of the process, as you may find that you have identified as the ideal positioning for your practice an area where many other organizations already compete. If you discover this early on, the only thing you need do is consider other positioning alternatives; too late, and you may find yourself unable to compete effectively in your chosen market niche.

Step #8. Select a strategic part of the positioning pie with which your organization wishes to be identified. The management of the consulting organization now must make a key decision: the final choice as to the overall strategic thrust of the positioning program that will be executed.

Step #9. Ensure that the positioning and its attendant positioning line are a good fit with the overall strategic direction of the company. Consider such things as the following:

- *The ability to deliver the positioning.* The best and most creative positioning is worth little if the organization cannot deliver what is promised.

- *The degree to which the message and the specific positioning line are meaningful to the target consumer.* This is absolutely essential, as the positioning must have significant appeal to the target customer for it to be effective.

- *The extent to which the ownership of the company is comfortable with the positioning.* The positioning must feel right from a very subjective point of view; it is a statement that the organization must be able to live with for some time.

After you have gone through these nine steps, you should have a positioning that constitutes a meaningful statement about the services of your organization *and* is appealing to the target customer.

EXECUTIONAL CONSIDERATIONS IN THE DEVELOPMENT OF A COMPANY IDENTITY

Developing a positioning for a consulting organization represents the strategic aspect of creating a company identity. It establishes an overall strategic framework for the more visible parts of the company identity. The balance of this chapter will identify the key executional elements that communicate the overall company identity to the outside world.

The Positioning Line

One of the most obvious ways that an organization communicates a company identity is through a slogan or series of words that clearly exemplifies its positioning. "The ultimate driving machine" (BMW), "We're a part of your life" (Macy's), "Don't leave home without it" (American Express), "The real thing" (Coke), "Squeezably soft" (Charmin)—these are all positioning lines, most or all of which probably are familiar to you.

The development of such a line is a creative process, and it is very difficult to do; in some cases, success is not possible. However, if you do manage to come up with something that is relatively short (i.e., less than seven to ten words), memorable, and captures the essence of the organization's positioning, the positioning line can be an integral part of your entire communications effort.

The Graphic Look

Another obvious way to communicate the company identity is visually, by developing a graphic look that articulates the feeling and the culture of your organization. This need not be elaborate, but it must be consistent with the message that you are trying to communicate to your target audience. A consultant who is beginning a practice in executive compensation counseling would probably have a graphic approach very different from that of a person who is beginning a consulting practice in graphic design, just as a real estate consulting business would have a very different graphic look from a practice that is providing consulting services in a field of medicine or science. In each case, logos, print styles, and colors send a message to the target audience about the type and character of the organization. The graphic approach should be a direct outgrowth of both the positioning strategy and the positioning line that have been developed in order to deliver a single, coherent message to the target audience.

The graphic look of the organization should be viewed as permanent, or at least very long term. The objective is to develop a durable graphic presentation of the business that will work for your organization ten years hence as well as it does today. Thus, the look of the company, its graphics, colors, or type styles, should not be trendy, or, when the fad passes, the company will look out-of-date or behind the times.

The graphic look also must be appropriate for a variety of different communications vehicles. Some organizations design very attractive four-color graphics that will look terrific on executive stationery, forgetting that the graphic mostly will be seen in black and white (as a result of photocopying or facsimile transmission), in a reduced format (business cards, bills, etc.), or on presentation folders, advertising specialty products, or other items that carry the company name.

The logo. The logo is the way the company name is communicated to the outside world. It involves the following elements:

- *The actual name that is used.* We will cover the selection of a name for your company later in this chapter; however, for the purpose of this section, the logo uses the name by which you wish to be called. For example, International Business Machines has chosen to use a logo that contains the letters IBM, Pepsi Cola uses Pepsi, and American Telephone & Telegraph uses a logo with the letters AT&T. In each of these cases, the letters in the logo have become the moniker for the company both within the internal organization and in the outside world.

- *The way the name is shown in the logo.* This refers to the graphics that are used for the name. For example, the type-style employed by Kraft is considerably different from that used by Audi or IBM or Coca Cola. Further, each of these logos has a different look than one might expect from a law firm, a physician, or the Internal Revenue Service. In each case, the way the name is written communicates a specific message to the reader and is a meaningful component of the overall company identity and graphic look.

It is worth noting that many major corporations spend thousands of dollars working with graphic design firms to determine the ideal typestyle for the letters in their names. While service or consulting businesses do not need to go that far, it is important to commit the right effort to identifying the typestyle that is most consistent with the overall image your organization is seeking to develop.

- *The use, or lack of use, of color in the logo.* The use of color in a logo for a consulting/service organization probably varies in importance according to the nature of the business. For example, a management consulting firm might choose to use black or very conservative, dark colors in its logo in order to communicate a specific message. On the other hand, a consulting company that offers graphic design, packaging, or interior design consulting might want to use multiple colors in the logo, while a company that offers consulting services on the environment might choose to reinforce that message with a logo that uses either blue or green.

- *The use of ancillary symbols in the logo.* Many organizations feel that they can add to the message and imagery of their logo by adopting a symbol that is always used with the name. For example, a marketing research company might incorporate a picture of a small telephone or a clipboard in its logo to reinforce the nature of its business; a sales consultant might include a volume chart showing an upward trend, and a cardiac rehabilitation center might reproduce a small segment of a healthy cardiogram to reinforce awareness of the nature of its business.

Some graphic design specialists feel that symbols are very helpful to differentiate one organization from another, whereas other people feel that symbols get in the way of communicating the name. This is an individual decision; however, my own experience is that symbols are generally not necessary in the logos of service or consulting businesses.

This is not to suggest that you should not use a very unique symbol that can become ownable by your company if you have developed one; rather, I am merely pointing out that the chances of any device of this nature contributing much to the overall communication and imagery of a consulting business are very limited.

One of the most important considerations that any organization must incorporate into its culture is the need for consistent use of the company name in all communications. It does not matter whether the organization is a one-person compensations consulting company or a fifty-person marketing research organization, this consistency must be sacrosanct. Specifically, this means that, whenever the name is used in external or internal communications, it must be shown in precisely the same way, relative to the logo type style and the colors. Furthermore, standards should be established as to what the organization will be called in oral communications. For example, often a company with a relatively long name adopts a nickname (say, CCG for Connecticut Consulting Group); however, the use of this abbreviation in the outside world should be determined based on the desires of management relative to the long-term company identity needs for the organization.

To illustrate how these principles can be applied—successfully or not—the following will analyse the logos of several companies that operate different types of consulting practices, in terms of what I believe are the strengths and weaknesses of each. I am not privy to the internal strategies of any of the organizations whose logos I discuss here; the commentary is based on my interpretation of the logo and how it fits with my perception of the companies.

McKinsey&Company, Inc.

Above is the logo of McKinsey & Company a leading management consulting firm. This is an example of a very simple logo that communicates the professional image of the company it represents. There are no gimmicks, nothing fancy—simply a very straightforward approach to presenting the name of the firm in a way that subtly communicates the esteemed position it holds in the management consulting industry.

The logo above is an example of the effective use of a memorable logo device to reinforce the identity of the organization. Santell Market Research is seeking to develop a unique and memorable identity for its services by incorporating the delta symbol in its logo. Since the marketing research industry has a quantitative orientation, the presence of the delta communicates the functional capabilities of the company (providing numerical data to clients).

On the other hand, the above presents an example of a logo that is confusing and relatively meaningless. All it communicates is the name of the principal of the firm, and the initials are both redundant and apparently pointless. Importantly, upon exposure to the logo, one does not have a clue as to the nature of the consulting practice—George J. Ciaccio & Associates (GJC&A) are safety and sales consultants—nor does one get a sense of the image or orientation of the business.

Three different logos for leading packaging design consultants are shown below. These three firms compete for essentially the same market: the package goods industry/consumer products container designs. All

stuart/gunn & furuta inc

three have chosen different approaches in their logos. Stuart/Gunn & Furuta Inc. has incorporated the initials of the named principals into a design logo that is used in association with the actual names. They communicate their creativity by the design approach they take to the letters in the name logo. In a somewhat similar fashion, Selame Design have utilized a very modern and artistic approach to incorporating the initial letters from Selame Design into a logo that clearly communicates creativity. This logo, however, has much greater interest value and memorability than does the Stuart/Gunn & Furuta logo.

Selame Design

The Peterson & Blyth logo takes a different approach altogether, in that it does not communicate creativity via its logo as the other two firms do. Apparently, this firms feels that its name is sufficiently strong to communicate the capabilities of the organization without other devices. It therefore communicates a more strategic and perhaps less creative approach to package design.

Peterson & Blyth Associates Inc.

Writing and presentation materials. Every consulting organization has a variety of different ways of communicating to its current clients and prospects, each of which must be viewed as part of the company identity.

- *The business card.* Your business card communicates a message about you, and, frequently, it is responsible for the first impression when you make an initial contact with a prospective client. Therefore, it is important to pay attention to certain details. The quality of the paper used in the business card conveys an impression. A very thin or a cheap-quality paper certainly sends a different message than does a heavy paper or a parchmentlike card. Raised letters, too, convey a very different image than do flat printed letters. Finally, the layout and the type of information on the business card communicates something about the company. For example, some service or consulting organizations include sales points on their business cards, while others feel that a very clean look, with simply the name, title, address, and phone number, is more appropriate to their overall image.

- *Company stationery.* Your stationery also communicates something important about the company identity that the organization is seeking to project. Several elements contribute to the image or company identity communicated by the stationery you use. How is the name used? Where it is placed? What other information is on the stationery in addition to the firm name, address, and telephone number? Paper makes a difference, too. Is it standard bond paper or something much more special/expensive? Do you use originals or photocopies for outside correspondence? Nowadays, many organizations retain originals for their records and send copies out to their correspondents. This sends a different message to the recipient than would the use of an original of the document.

- *Binders and other presentation materials.* One of the most visible parts of a company identity in the consulting business is your initial presentation when you come to sell a prospect on your services. Several different elements of this presentation contribute to the overall company identity that you will communicate to the prospect.

What is the look of the presentation? In a later chapter, I will talk about the content of the presentation; at this point, the physical appearance is of concern. Does it look professional, representative of the type of work that the client might get from the consultant in a final report, or is it disorganized, appearing to have been thrown together hastily?

What is the format of presentation? Is it presented in a binder, on 35-mm slides, in acetates, or on loose pieces of paper? Each of these approaches can be effective, if presented professionally, but they all communicate a different image of the style and professionalism of the consulting organization.

Do the covers/binders for your leave-behind materials (if any) and your final reports effectively convey the image of your organization? It is important to remember that the end product of many consulting engagements is a long written report that will remain on the client's shelf (for all to see) for some time to come. You should take care to design a report cover that you would be proud to see in someone's office and that will contribute to the name recognition of your practice.

The Office Environment

Yet another important part of the overall company image/identity relates to the offices where your business is located. The location of your office communicates a message to clients, particularly in cases where clients come to you. Many consultants who start out in their own one-man-band businesses begin by working from their homes to minimize their start-up costs. Students in my courses are always asking if this is advisable. In my judgment, a consulting business can be successfully run from the home or from an office, but you must resolve the following questions about a home office before choosing that route.

Are you opting for a home office because you are not confident about your success and so want to minimize risk? If so, this attitude might be apparent to your clients and prospects, which will not be in the best interest of the business.

Have you chosen a home office because your commitment to the business is not full time: If this is the situation (which could be completely valid for some types of consulting), then you must ask yourself whether this will be transparent to your clients and prospects, most of whom would prefer a consultant with a long-term commitment to the business. Further, and of perhaps greater importance, is your mental and emotional commitment to your own business if you view it as a part-time venture. Will you put enough physical and emotional energy into the business to make it work under these conditions?

Is it possible for you to go to work when your office is at home? This is one of the biggest problems facing people with offices in their homes.

They often have trouble changing from their social selves to their work selves. Some begin working much later and stop much earlier than they might do otherwise; others always are finding excuses to run out to the refrigerator for a quick snack; still others find that they become responsible for babysitting, receiving shipments of furniture or other purchases, or performing other household tasks. This would not happen if the office were out of the home.

Perhaps the best way to address this whole issue is to ask yourself if you can really provide a businesslike environment in your home office. This often depends on whether clients will come to your office or you use it only as your work facility. If clients expect to come to your office, then you probably will have to duplicate an outside office in your home, complete with such things as a waiting room, a conference area, a receptionist, and so on. If the office is only for you, a much more sparse environment would be acceptable.

If you have made the decision to have an office outside the home, you must decide what type of location you would find to be the most appropriate.

A large number of start-up consultants choose to rent a small office in a large office building, as it is relatively easy to find a space of the right size. This environment offers the benefits of a credible location (i.e., with other professionals) and the opportunity to sound out other businesses in the area as potential clients. There are, however, some disadvantages to this situation. One often has to commit to a long-term lease in a large building, which may be a problem if the business grows and requires more space. Also, in a large building, it is more difficult to use the office environment to help establish a company character than it might be in a different, more unique location.

A very common way for a new consultant to start out is to rent space in an executive complex, where one gets an office in a very attractive suite and has access (on a per diem basis) to secretarial help, copying machines, conference rooms, and so forth. This type of situation can be very convenient, as you can start up a business immediately in an office environment that is professional looking and ready for business. The disadvantage is that this arrangement looks, feels, and is temporary, which can affect the overall emotional commitment that you give to the venture. If you feel the business is temporary and might not work, then, subconsciously, you might take a different approach to building your clientele. Because the location communicates "temporary" to clients, they might not want to become involved with you, thinking that you are likely not to stay long.

Another choice popular with a large number of consultants is to locate the office in a small building or a converted home. This is often a very good solution for the new consultant; often, many very economical spaces are available, and, frequently, the individual can get more space than is really needed for the same price that he or she would have paid in a very large building. As a result, the consultant can expand the practice without moving to a second location. Another key advantage is that this arrangement often enables the consultant to find a space with a unique character, such as a converted farm house or an old mansion. This type of office environment can add to the overall company image that is conveyed by the organization.

Another issue that a consultant faces when setting up a business is where to establish an office. Should it be in a large city where there are lots of different businesses or in a small suburban location close to home? Where you begin your business can have an impact on the overall image of the organization, whether you want this or not. A personnel consulting company located in Westport, Connecticut, conveys a different image than does one on Park Avenue in New York City or in Easton, Pennsylvania. Some of the key issues that relate to the decisions regarding where to establish your business follow:

- If clients frequently come to your offices, it is probably a good idea to choose a location that is convenient for them, in terms of access to transportation. Similarly, if the bulk of your clientele is likely to be located in one city, then you probably should have your offices there or very nearby.

- The extent to which you require the support of outside subcontracting services also could have a significant impact on your choice of a location for your business. For example, if your business requires the use of artists, graphic designers, or printing facilities, you probably will want to be very close to these resources.

- Your own desired lifestyle is also a very important consideration. One of the major reasons that people go into their own consulting businesses is to have control over their lifestyles.

Consequently, a great many people establish offices near their homes, so that they do not have to commute long distances to work, while others locate their offices near recreational facilities or other similar attractions.

Once you have decided on an office, you should consider what sort of environment you wish to establish in it. The way you decorate the office will communicate a great deal about the atmosphere that exists within the organization and the type of company it is. This is not to suggest that you should emphasize the external, more superficial aspects of the business but rather to indicate that they do play an important part in setting the tone for the practice. The use of new or very old furniture, its style, the way the entire place is decorated—the light, the wall decorations, carpeting and so on—and the existence of private offices or partitions for the staff all send a message about the kind of company you run.

The total amount of space that you commit to in your office also can communicate something about the nature of your company. If clients walk into an office that is very cramped, with people sitting right next to each other, they will get one image. On the other hand, if the office is so spacious that there is considerable waste, clients might think that they are paying extra fees to cover the high costs of the space.

A very important part of the company identity and overall image of some consulting organizations is the tone that is established in the office. It affects the feelings both of outsiders and also of the people who work in the company.

A key element of office tone is office dress in terms of the relative degree of formality (or informality) of the various people in the organization. Some people in the consulting business feel that they must be very formal, with both men and women professionals in dark suits and the support staff dressed as they would be in a major metropolitan area legal office. Others conform to much more informal dress standards and believe that this contributes to a better work ethic. Whatever the approach, the person entering a consulting business should make a decision in full recognition that whatever he or she establishes will have an impact on the overall culture of the organization and will be very difficult to change once the pattern has been set.

Office interpersonal communications also constitute a very important part of the overall office character or image. If the office staff address the professionals by their first names, this will establish a different feeling in the office than if they use Mr. and Ms.

A final area worth mentioning is the extent to which people in the office socialize during nonbusiness hours. While there is very little the owner of a business can do to stop socializing among employees (should this be a concern), there is a great deal that can be done to foster it. For example, if the management of a consulting company holds social occasions with the staff, this will send a message that office socializing is an encouraged activity. Others likely will follow, and the result will be a social subculture within the organization. This may or may not be desirable for the business; the point is that the owner does have some influence in this area, if only in one direction.

The Name

One of the questions that is asked most frequently by students seeking to set up their own consulting businesses is how important a role the name plays in the company identity of their business. Some people agonize more over the selection of the name for their practice than they do over most of the key strategic decisions they have to make relative to the elements of the marketing mix. However, while I feel that the name of the consulting company can be very important, I believe that it offers more of a downside risk than an upside opportunity. For example, an exceptional name is unlikely to have much positive impact on the ultimate success of the consulting practice. On the other hand, a name that is simply inappropriate could affect the growth of your business adversely, at least in the short term. Thus, you should be very careful when you select the name for your organization. For one thing, the company name generally is permanent, making it very difficult, inconvenient, and frequently expensive to change. Your clients, suppliers, bankers, and prospects will get to know you by your name. If you decide to change it, you will first have to inform the various groups that come in contact with your organization about the new name. The communication of this change must be accomplished very effectively over an extended period of time, as it is more difficult to register a new name for an existing consulting company than it is to develop awareness of a new brand name. Furthermore, when you change the name of your company, people will want a reasonable explanation of the reason for the change. The assumption will be that the name change is due to some major strategic change in the company or, at least, to significant additions to the staff or functional capabilities. Finally, you will need to replace all old communication items, such as stationery, bills, business cards, and the like, with ones that contain the new name. This process can be very expensive.

Another thing that you must remember is that your name is an articulation of your company personality. Many organizations use the company name to position themselves in the industry. The name represents your first impression in a vast majority of situations. When you first make contact with prospective clients, bankers, or suppliers they will hear (or see) your company name before almost anything else. This will create an impression in their minds, that could have a significant effect on how they perceive your services during the crucial first few minutes of the initial meeting. For example, if you run a secondary marketing research company named FastFacts, you create a different impression if the same organization were called Analytical Services, Inc. Both names could serve companies well in the same business, but what their names communicate about the nature of their practices is significantly different. The name is how you will refer to your company and what others will call you. Clearly, it must be very comfortable to you—it is something you will hear very frequently.

The task of selecting a name for your organization can be accomplished relatively easily, if you follow the proven process described below that covers the necessary steps that will lead to a satisfactory end result.

Step #1. Develop a name selection strategy. The first, and most important, part of the entire name selection process is the development of a strategy statement that will provide the overall criteria for determining the ultimate appropriateness of a name. This statement should be a brief, *written* document that establishes the key philosophical points that relate to the name of your organization. The name selection strategy should cover several areas. First, what do you want your company name to accomplish? Among the most common alternatives, you might want the name to do the following:

- Communicate to prospective customers your personal name. To achieve this, you might adopt your own name for the company (e.g., Larry G. Peters Consulting).

- Describe the type of business you are operating (e.g., Promotional Consulting Corporation or Executive Personal Placement Inc.).

- Communicate how you do your business (e.g., Quik Facts Inc. or Taxfast).

- Send a message to a specific target audience (e.g., Radio Research, Inc., or Beverage Sales Consultants).

The strategy should indicate how and where the name will be used. If you operate the type of consulting company that will be producing a great many mailings, advertisements, or advertising specialties that include your name, this should be mentioned in the strategy, as it could be a factor in the name that you select. The strategy also should provide some indication as to whether the name should be short or long, one word or several, consist of real words or use contrived ones (e.g., Kodak, Xerox) that will evolve to become your identity.

Step #2.   Gives others copies of your name strategy and ask them for suggestions as to possible choices for your company name. Most people enjoy participating in this type of exercise and will willingly give a little time to the process of thinking about a name for your company. The key is to seek input from many different people and to make sure that no judgments are made on any submissions until all are received.

Step #3.   Develop an alphabetical list of all name candidates and begin to make some subjective judgments. Simply review all the names that have been given to you and eliminate those that do not match the criteria or just do not feel correct. This is a very important part of the process, as it is the first major step in which the number of potential names is reduced to a manageable amount.

Step #4.   Select the leading candidates and briefly list the strengths and weaknesses of each. This process should eliminate more of the candidates, as you may find some names have too many weaknesses and not enough strengths or that some have one overriding weakness that precludes even considering the strengths.

Step #5. Make a list of three to five finalist names and ask friends and colleagues for their opinions about the best alternatives. While in the ideal world, one might consider conducting some quantitative or qualitative market research to evaluate the reactions of target customers to these names, in most start-up consulting practices, there simply are not sufficient funds for this. Consequently, it is advisable to expose the name to others in your personal and business circles to obtain their reactions. Keep track of the various opinions that are expressed and consider all of them in the final analysis.

Step #6. Select the name that feels right in light of all the inputs received. In most cases, what feels right at this stage will be the correct name for you; however, before you adopt it, you will want to ask yourself the following questions:

1. Is the name easy to pronounce and simple to remember?

2. Does the name come across effectively on the telephone?

3. Does the name lend itself to the overall strategic positioning of the organization and is it consistent with the feel and tone of the other parts of the marketing mix?

4. Is it possible (or even just likely) that the name could cause your organization to be confused with another company in your industry?

Step #7. Check out the legality of the name. Once you have chosen a name for your organization, it is vital that you retain a lawyer to conduct a trademark search, to ensure that someone else does not have your name or one that is dangerously similar. This is very important; there have been dozens of cases in recent years of organizations that introduce products or services under one name, only to find out that they must abandon the effort because of a conflict with some other name already in use.

Many ask why it is necessary to go through such a formal process to select a name, particularly when one is beginning a small consulting business and does not contemplate adding more people to the organization for some time to come. Clearly, it is possible to develop an effective name for your organization without going through a formal process; however, there are some very excellent reasons to follow the steps that have just been outlined. First, the formality of the process will force you to think through the various key issues that should be considered whenever you select something this important for the business. The process also encourages creativity, as it encourages you to think about alternative names that might be desirable. Moreover, it provides an opportunity for you to gain outside input that might prove to be extremely helpful. Finally, it ensures that the name that you ultimately select has been chosen because of a conscious effort on your part to evaluate the strengths and weaknesses of all the alternatives that were proposed.

Whenever the subject of name selection comes up in the classroom, two key points require significant additional discussion. First of all, while it is very common for service businesses to adopt the name(s) of their founder(s), what are the advantages and drawbacks associated with this choice?

One advantage of using your own name for the company is that it is an ego experience, reinforced on a daily basis. This is very important to some people, and for many, it is one of the major reasons why they choose to start their own businesses. Others like to use their names because this gives them and their companies instant recognition. This is only true, however, if your name is well known. If you were (are) a famous athlete, musician, politician, or business person, it might be much to your advantage to lend your name to the company. However, if your name is not well known, the effect of using your name can be detrimental. Finally, naming the company after yourself also has the distinct advantage of identifying you as the boss, which may be very important to you relative to both internal company and external client issues.

There are also some important disadvantages associated with using your name as the name of the company. Perhaps the biggest is that it may make the business sound small, even to the extent that it communicates to the target that you are operating a one-man company. Another problem is that many clients or suppliers will want to work only with you. Also, the use of your name as the company identifier may make it much more difficult for you eventually to sell the equity you have built in the company—the value of a company called Executive Financial Planning Consultants will almost always have more inherent value than an identical company named Peter G. Lester, Inc. Similarly, it is dramatically more difficult for the founder of a self-named company to offer the outside world a believable line of succession; the company will still appear to represent you by virtue of the fact that it bears your name.

The second issue relates to using a descriptive name instead. Such a name can be excellent or very bad, depending on the nature of the industry and the actual name that is selected. The name must be very consistent with your overall company strategy and image. You must be very careful not to select a name that is too cute, too confusing, or too difficult to understand. Also, the name must be very different from others in the industry, or confusion will result.

SUMMARY

The company identity you develop for your consulting practice is an extremely important part of your marketing plan. The key to this process is to consider all the factors that contribute to the establishment of a company identity, such as positioning, the graphic look, the office tone and environment, and the name.

6 Planning Your Company's Finances

The principal problem that most new consulting practices have in the early months (and years) of operation is cash flow. Many consultants have left the profession because they simply could not generate the cash flow to pay their bills and then have sufficient monies left over to pay themselves a reasonable wage. The use of the term *cash flow*, rather than fees or revenues, is deliberate; it is possible to generate significant revenues without being able to collect the monies owed, thereby creating a cash availability problem.

This chapter will provide information that will help you determine how to set your fees and what programs need to be put into place to enable you to generate the cash flow needed to pay bills and salaries. This information is not intended to replace the advice of a qualified accountant but to serve as a guide to understanding the key issues that you will need to discuss in detail with your financial advisor when you establish your consulting business.

FEES

Setting fees is generally one of the most difficult problems that consultants face. You must be able to charge enough to generate sufficient revenues to meet the cash flow and personal income requirements; however, at the same time, your pricing structure should be low enough so that you do not lose assignments because of price.

Pricing Theory

The following section will discuss several different theoretical approaches to pricing consulting services. All are used successfully every day by consultants in different disciplines, and often the same consultant might follow several different approaches, depending on the scope of the assignment, the competitive environment in which he or she is involved, or the nature of the client organization. You should become familiar with each of the following approaches and then determine which makes the most sense for your practice, in light of the objectives that you have established.

Trial strategy. A common practice of many consultants is to price the first assignment very low, in order to be retained for the job. The theory behind this approach is that, once the client organization works with the consultant, it will appreciate his or her value and be receptive to a later fee increase because of price/value relationship that has been established.

The biggest advantage of this approach to pricing is that it will enable the consultant to secure more contracts than he or she might otherwise get, and this is particularly important to the new consultant who is trying to build an impressive client list. For this reason, some consultants adopt the trial strategy of pricing in the early months of the practice. However, this approach also suffers from some disadvantages, which some consultants find to be so serious, that they will not use this pricing methodology. The most significant disadvantages are:

- *The loss of income during the course of the first engagement.* Some consultants feel that they should not lose (or work at reduced rates) on any assignment, even in the early months of the business when their objective is to build a client list.

- *The difficulty of raising fees later, after the precedent of the first assignment.* In theory, a price increase will be easier once a client experiences the quality of work of the consultant; in practice, however, it frequently is not. This is because the client organization associates you with a specific fee structure and often will have difficulty accepting the rationale for a higher-level fee.

- *The price/quality image that can be created.* If you turn in the lowest bid for an assignment, prospective clients may look on you as a lower-quality consulting service. Your low bid may get this first assignment, but it may also tarnish your image in the prospect universe, which may hurt your chances of future assignments.

A frequently employed approach to the trial pricing strategy is to sell services in very small, individually priced segments, so that the client's absolute financial outlay is low, but the consultant sacrifices neither the current profitability nor the future possibility of receiving appropriate fees. In my experience, most client organizations are very favorable toward this approach (particularly in new relationships), as it enables both parties to get to know one another on a low-cost assignment before either make a significant commitment.

Maximum profit strategy. In this approach, the consultant establishes the pricing for an assignment based on what the consultant feels he or she can get for it, not on a specific hourly or daily rate. The fee is thus a function of the perceived value of the services to the client organization. Implicit in this approach is a belief that the hourly rate earned on the assignment will be greater than what the consultant would normally receive.

The advantage of this approach is that it makes each assignment very profitable for the consultant. This places somewhat less pressure on the consultant to sell new projects. However, this approach may not work in competitive situations, since others often will submit lower bids. Also, it is often difficult to provide a rationale for fees charged, if the client organization asks. This may create significant problems during the assignment or in the future. Finally, it is almost impossible to maintain consistency of pricing relative to future assignments because there is no statistical basis for the fee charged.

Pricing to competition. Some consulting organizations base their entire pricing strategy on the competitive situation, and they communicate this to prospective clients by several different means. Specifically, they indicate that they will meet the pricing of any major competitor, as long as the scope of the proposals is identical; they also state in their proposals that the hourly (or daily) rate that they charge is based on the standards of their competitors, and that their objective is to be equal to them. Other consultants seek to be the least (or most) expensive among the consultants with whom they normally compete for business.

While a pricing policy that considers the competitive situation can be very advantageous, it is essential for consultants that follow a parity-pricing philosophy to ensure that they offer the same scope of consulting services to the prospect organization as does their competition.

Pricing for continuity. Another common approach to pricing consulting services is to establish a base price that is acceptable to both parties (typically expressed in terms of an hourly or daily rate) and then to hold that rate for an extended period of time. Consultants generally follow this approach with clients with whom they have ongoing relationships, whereas they might adopt a trial pricing strategy with new clients. As long as the consultant keeps his rates at the same level, pricing will not be a major issue with the client organization. This constitutes the advantage of this approach, in that the consultant does not have to justify his fees continually to the client organization. At the same time, however, the consultant has no easy way to increase pricing when necessary. As a result, an engagement well into a relationship often will be less profitable than if one reviewed the pricing structure at the beginning of each project.

Approaches to Pricing Consulting Assignments

Within the consulting business, there are essentially three different ways to bill for consulting services: by project, with a retainer, and per diem.

Project basis. The project basis is an approach whereby the client and the consultant define a specific assignment and the consultant works exclusively on that project for a specific fee. Because the fee is determined before the project is begun, the cost to the client does not depend on the amount of work that is required to finish the task. Examples of consulting projects that might be suitable for this type of pricing arrangement include

- Development of a personnel policy for relocation of company employees
- Development of a reporting and control system for a sales organization
- Development of a computer software package that will enable the client organization to track more effectively the cost of providing customer service calls
- Implementation of four focus groups for a bank seeking information on consumer attitudes toward their new advertising campaign

The project system defines the scope of the work that is required so that the client cannot request help from the consultant in another area without incurring additional costs. Also, it enables the consultant to estimate the revenues and profitability of the project before the work even has begun. Finally, it provides an excellent incentive to the consultant to complete the work ahead of schedule, as this would make the project more profitable.

From the client's perspective, the project system controls the expenses of hiring the consultant and focuses the consultant's attention on one very specific project that can be defined in such a way that the client will be able to measure the contribution that the consultant makes to the organization.

The disadvantages of the project system for the consultant are that it places a major premium on the consultant's ability to price a consulting assignment properly. Also, it often puts the consultant in an uncomfortable position, as people in the client organization often will ask for assistance in areas that are beyond the scope of the assignment and expect these extra services to be included in the project fee. Finally, it generally does not offer the consultant as great an opportunity to identify other potential assignments within the client organization as would other types of fee arrangements.

The project system does not enable the client organization to benefit from the overall capabilities of the consultant, because of the focus on one project area of the client's business. Also, the client may have to overpay for the work if the consultant can complete the assignment more quickly than was anticipated.

Retainer basis. A retainer is a consulting arrangement whereby a client organization hires the consultant for a specified period of time (normally six months or one year) during which the consultant is expected to work for the client on a variety of different projects. Normally, a retainer is based on the consultant providing the client organization with a specific amount of time (e.g., three days per month) which becomes the basis for the cost of the retainer.

Retainer arrangements can be open- or closed-ended. In a closed-ended retainer, the client and consultant agree on a list of projects that are to be completed during the term of the retainer. Typically, this list will include many different types of assignments with specific deadlines.

If the retainer is open-ended, the consultant provides services to the client organization on an as-needed basis, in whatever areas where help is needed. The projects generally are not identified specifically at the start of the arrangement. Usually, however, there is a general idea of the major tasks for which the consultant will be responsible, while other projects will be executed as the need arises.

For the consultant, the advantages of the retainer system are that it provides a predictable source of revenue for an extended period of time. The consultant thus can plan his or her time (or that of the others in the organization) more effectively because of the guaranteed revenue from the retainer.

A retainer generally enables the consultant to become involved in many different areas of the client's business, which normally will make the contribution on each project more valuable (due to the overall organizational perspective). With a retainer arrangement, it normally is not necessary for the client to update the consultant on each new project, because of the consultant's general familiarity with the on-going business.

This involvement also enables the consultant to identify new areas of potential involvement for new business. These new projects can expand the size of the current retainer or expand the length of the retainer beyond the agreed time frame.

Under a retainer arrangement, the client, too, benefits from the consultant's involvement in several/many different areas of the business, because this allows the client to leverage the consultant's time more effectively. Also, the cost of the consultant's services is predictable for the length of the contract.

The disadvantages of the retainer arrangement for the consultant are that the client organization can place unfair time demands on the consultant yet expect that the work will be accomplished for the same fee. Also, with retainer arrangements, some clients feel they own the consultant, expecting them to be available on a moment's notice twenty-four hours per day, 7 days per week. They often are not very understanding of the consultant's schedule vis-à-vis other clients.

As for the client organization, it may receive relatively little work for the retainer fee if it does not manage the consultant effectively. The consultant gets paid regardless of the amount of work implemented on behalf of the client organization.

Per diem arrangement. In a per diem arrangement, the consultant and the client agree to a fee schedule (on a daily or hourly basis), and the consultant then bills the client only for the time incurred on its behalf.

The advantages of the per diem system are that the consultant gets paid for all his or her time. Also, under this arrangement, each hour of consultant time is billable and easily identifiable, so the client is less likely to use the consultant for menial or insignificant projects.

For the client, the advantage is the consultant only charges for the precise time spent working on their project. Also, some clients prefer the per diem arrangement because it offers them greater control over the cost of consultants: The client has the ability to stop the consultant at any time or at the cost ceiling it requires.

The per diem arrangement can work against the consultant. The client organization may be less likely to call on the services of the consultant because of the direct costs associated with using that individual. As a result, the total fees that the consultant generates from the client organization may be less than what might otherwise have been realized. Another problem with this type of arrangement is that the consultant becomes very accountable for every hour or day spent on the client's business. The consultant keeps excellent track of his or her time, in order to be able to answer any questions regarding fees.

From the clients' perspective, the per diem arrangement can reward inefficiency, since the consultant gets paid on a time basis regardless of how efficiently he or she performed the work. Also, the client does not have as much control over the cost of the consultant's services, since the fees are incurred on an open-ended basis.

Considerations in Establishing Consulting Fee Structures

A variety of different factors will determine the most appropriate fee arrangements for your consulting organization. The relative importance of each of these will differ by type of consulting practice, individual consultants' financial needs and expectations, area of the country, and, possibly, by the time of year.

Competitive environment. One key consideration in pricing your services is the fees charged by the competition. If your direct competitors charge clients $1500 per day, it probably would not be in your best interest to vary from that amount by more than 15 to 20 percent unless you have a very strong justification for the difference.

Internal cost structure. You must consider your own costs of doing business when developing a pricing structure for your consulting practice. This includes such things as salaries, rents, operating expenses, and other costs directly associated with running the business.

Client value. You should also consider the added value that your services will bring to the client organization. This value can range from direct monetary benefits that the client will gain from your involvement to the loss of opportunities that they will experience if they do not hire you. If you are in the business of correcting problems, you might be able to charge very large fees because, without your help, the client cannot run the basic business properly.

Your own income and time criteria. Some consultants will not work unless they can get a specific hourly rate. Others intentionally price assignments high because they want to work relatively few hours but earn significant monies. By pricing their services high, they only get the most profitable assignments.

The current state of your business. In many situations, the amount of work that you have at a given time will have a definite impact on the pricing structure that you employ at that time. For example, if you are very busy, the price for a new assignment will often be higher than if you are really in need of work.

A Hypothetical Model for Establishing Fees

This model will help you determine what the normal daily rate should be for your services. Once this rate is established, it is much easier to make specific adjustments upward or downward based on other considerations (i.e., the competition, value to the client, prestige value of the client, consultant's own workload, etc.) that must figure into any pricing decision. It would be impossible for this model to apply equally well to every type of consulting practice, but virtually any consultant will be able to modify the formula to make it apply to their specific practices.

Defining a working day.   I believe that every consultant must define what a day means in terms of the number of hours it contains. Is a day at the client's office any significant block of time spent on the premises, or must the consultant be there for a specific number of hours to qualify for one billing day?

For the purpose of this model, let's assume that one consulting day equals eight hours of work on behalf of the client. Depending on the policies of the consultant, this may or may not include the time required to travel from the consultant's home or office to the client's premises. There are excellent arguments in favor of both sides of this question, and the consultant simply must determine what definition is most comfortable for him or her.

Defining the number of working days in a year.   The number of working days in a year can be anything up to 365, or maybe even more, if a working day is only 8 hours but the consultant puts in 10 to 12 hours per day (i.e., 1.5 billing days). In most situations, I recommend assuming that a working year for a consultant consists of approximately 230 days, derived as follows:

Total number of days in the year		365
Less		
Weekends	104	
Holidays	9	
Vacation	15	
Administrative and sick days	7	
Subtotal		135
Working days		230

Identifying expenses.   The third step in the process is to identify the costs incurred to operate the business. The following represent the categories considered in this hypothetical model:

Rent	$10,000
Secretary	
(salary plus fringes and bonus)	25,000
Assistant	
(salary plus fringes and bonus)	30,000
Travel	5,000
Office supplies	25,000
Total expenses	$95,000

Determining a personal income target.   Assuming that you want to make a salary of $85,000 plus approximately 25 percent to use for bonuses, benefits, and other related costs, you arrive at a personal income need of about $105,000.

Identifying the fixed costs.   If you add the business expenses to the personal income target, you get the base amount that the business must cover, in this case, $200,000.

Setting the standard fee.   If you divide the $200,000 in expenses by the 230 working days, you quickly arrive at a daily billing rate of $870. However, this rate is only accurate if the consultant bills 100 percent of the available time, which simply is never the case. In most practices, consultants can bill no more than 60 to 70 percent of the available time because of the normal downtime for training and development, business development, and inefficiency. Therefore, if we assume that this hypothetical consultant is very efficient and works 70 percent of the available time, then the billing rate necessary to generate $200,000 in revenue is $1,243 per day ($870/.70). If the consultant finds it impossible to justify a $1,243 billing rate and feels that the target audience would be much more receptive to something in the range of $800 per day, he or she must make one of the following decisions:

- Accept a lower level of personal income

- Reduce costs by not having an assistant or by working in his or her own home, or some similar effort

- Work evenings and weekends in order to expand the total number of billable days in a week, which will permit a lower daily rate, assuming that days are measured in hours of work against a particular assignment

Establishing what the fee includes. You have now established a fee for your services, but unless you spell out to the client precisely what the fee covers, problems may develop. You need to specify whether you or the client pays for such things as travel costs, express mail/messengers, long distance telephone calls, and business-related entertainment/meals. These costs can add up to very large amounts, and it is normal in many consulting businesses for the client to pick up these costs *in addition* to the fees that they are charged.

BILLINGS AND COLLECTIONS

There is a very important axiom in the consulting business: "If you do not collect the fees you generate, you will surely go out of business." My experience in the service industry suggests that collections problems are often one of the biggest issues that face a small business, as most people are very reluctant to pressure their clients to pay their bills, for fear of losing the relationship. However, it is very important to recognize that clients are as responsible for paying their bills (promptly!) as you are for providing quality consulting services to their organizations.

There are several different measures that consultants should take to ensure that they collect most or all of the monies owed to them by client organizations.

1. Develop strong internal controls to track the status of collections and to go after fees that are due. Vital to any accounting system in a consulting business is the ability to bill clients as soon as possible after the work is finished. If you maintain an active billing

tickler file, which you constantly update to keep track of when specific phases of projects are completed (and, therefore, when bills can be sent), the business will not get behind in its billings. You should also adopt a policy of telephoning all clients that are overdue in their payments to determine the nature of the problem and when payment will be made. Some people in the consulting business are against this practice since they feel it impacts negatively on the consulting relationship; however, my experience is that this policy can be handled very well (i.e., accounting department to accounting department) and can help significantly to avoid having to carry old receivables.

2. Establish a policy of billing clients in advance for assignments. Many consultants will not begin an assignment until they get paid for the initial part of the work. Most clients will accept this policy, as they recognize that consultants incur some operating expenses in executing assignments and require some fees at the beginning. It is not unusual to bill one-third to one-half of the fee for a project or the first quarter of a retainer at the time the contract is signed. In the case of a project, another third would be payable when the project is two-thirds done, with the balance due upon successful completion.

3. Refrain from paying directly for any client expenses, unless this is absolutely necessary. A consultant often implements work (e.g., research, printing, purchase of outside services, etc.) that is a direct client out-of-pocket expense and must decide whether to pay for it and then bill the client or to submit the bills directly to the client. Unless the consultant has a policy of marking up all out-of-pocket costs like those that go through his billing system (a practice I do not recommend), bills for these expenses should always be sent directly to the client for payment so they do not affect the cash flow of your company.

FINANCIAL CONTROL REPORTS

Some other key financial reports will help in the financial aspects of the practice. These reports fall into two principal categories: planning documents and operating documents.

Planning Documents

You should consider developing several key planning documents in the course of establishing your consulting business.

Revenue forecast. This document shows the projected revenue for each month during a year. It should be developed for the annual plan and then updated on a monthly basis throughout the year. The most sophisticated revenue forecasts include the sources of revenue, broken out by one or more of the following categories:

- Revenue from existing clients versus revenue from new clients
- Anticipated revenue by specific client
- Revenue by type of project
- Revenue by nature of relationship (i.e., retainers, projects, or per diems)

The revenue forecast is an extremely helpful planning tool for two key reasons. First, it causes the consultant to estimate at the beginning of the planning cycle the amount of business that will be generated during the year. This provides a sanity check—when the consultant looks at the total revenues that need to be generated and what has been achieved in the past, realism can step in and modify the projections.

Secondly, during the year this projection allows the consultant to monitor how the actual revenues compare to the original estimates. The consultant thus receives a snapshot view of the business's status at various times during the year and can make adjustments in expense planning or in revenue generation programs if needed.

Expense forecast. You should also place major importance on developing an annual and month-by-month projection of the expenses that will be incurred by your business during the year. This forecast will be based on the prior year's activities (for an ongoing business) and on the expenses associated with the elements of the marketing program. The expense forecast should be as detailed as possible to permit the business to identify where the actual expenses are deviating from the plan. This will be much more helpful when management of the company must determine where adjustments should be made.

Cash flow forecast.   Perhaps the most important planning document of all, the cash flow forecast projects the expenses (i.e., salaries, rent, utilities, etc.) that the business will pay and the revenues that the business will actually receive. With this analysis, it becomes possible to predict when cash shortfalls will occur and to seek extra sources of capital to meet the cash requirements. To be effective, however, this document *must* be updated on a monthly basis throughout the year, as the management of the consulting practice needs to know at all times what the requirements are for cash.

Operating Documents

A consulting business should also generate certain reports on a regular basis during the year, in order to manage the business effectively and profitably.

Monthly update of the planning documents.   Each month, you should update the revenue, expense, and cash flow forecasts with actual data.

Profit-and-loss statement.   On a quarterly basis (at least), you should develop a profit and loss statement showing how much money your company is making (or losing), both for the period being analyzed and to date for the year.

Aging of receivables.   The aging of receivables report shows all outstanding invoices that have been sent to clients, as well as their status in terms of how overdue they are, for what reasons they are overdue, what actions are being taken to collect the monies, and what the trend is in receivables (e.g., are the 60-day receivables growing?). This vital report ties in very closely with the cash flow forecast.

Revenues booked but not invoiced.   This report consists of a summary by the client of any revenue/time that has been booked but for which no invoice has been sent. The key is to find out why the client has not been invoiced, so that appropriate actions can be taken.

FINANCIAL ARRANGEMENTS WITH SUBCONTRACTORS

Virtually every type of consultant uses subcontractors to execute some client assignments. This practice raises several questions. First, should you mark up subcontractor services to your clients? If so, by how much? Those who believe that it is appropriate to mark up subcontractor services (normally by 10 to 17.5 percent) consider this to be a viable source of additional revenue, because they find the subcontractors and guarantee their work. They feel that they should be compensated for accepting these risks and that marking up subcontractor services is a relatively invisible way of handling this. Those who do not mark up these services want to demonstrate to clients that their selection of subcontractors is objective and feel that, if the consultant does not have any financial stake in the decision, it will be in the best interest of the client. Also, they do not want to be beholden to any subcontractors and so choose not to make money from this source. Finally, they want to maintain a high degree of professional integrity and feel that, while they should be paid for the time they spend supervising subcontractors, marking up these services is not the way to proceed.

Second, should you accept finder's fees from subcontractors? Organizations that accept these fees feel that it is common practice in their segment of the industry and, that they, too, have a right to benefit from this profit opportunity. Also, because they do not ask for the fees, they see nothing wrong in accepting them. Organizations that choose not to accept finder's fees do so because they want to be objective with regard to the suppliers they choose for their clients, and they believe that this would be difficult if a financial gain was associated with the decision. Also, they have a general feeling that this practice is not ethical, unless the client is aware of the situation. Finally, they feel that accepting finder's fees is cheapening, not unlike accepting a bribe.

Last, should you pay subcontractors yourself or have them bill your clients directly? Consultants who choose to pay subcontractors and then bill clients feel that this gives them better control over the situation, as they can be sure that the client is billed the correct amount. Some consultants insist on this practice, because it is the only way that they can mark up the subcontractor's services. Consultants that like subcontractors to bill clients directly feel that this communicates clearly to the client that the consultant is not making money from the use of subcontractor services. Also, this practice precludes the need to carry the costs of the subcontractor in the books while waiting for reimbursement from the client—in effect, it is an excellent help to their cash flow.

SUMMARY

This chapter has been about the basic issue of making money. Many people are excellent at selling consulting services but have considerable trouble generating enough revenues to meet expenses or have difficulty collecting the fees that are generated. To them this will be the most important chapter in the book.

The financial basics associated with operating a consulting practice are relatively simple. Charge an appropriate fee and collect the money that is owed to you. If you study this chapter and follow the suggested guidelines, you will be in an excellent position to benefit from the balance of this book, which provides the nuts and bolts of selling your services and servicing your clients.

Part 2
Implementation

7 Building Awareness of Your Business— Direct Methods

In the twenty years that I have been involved in marketing and sales, one consistent factor has been the extreme importance of generating awareness for a product or service. There are two different types of awareness; each is generated somewhat differently, and each plays a unique role in the marketing program for a product or service.

The most important is *unaided awareness*, defined as top-of-mind recall of a product or service. For example, if you were asked to identify five public accounting firms in the United States, whether you were able to name one, two, or all five, the ones you named would be recalled as a result of unaided awareness. They were on the top of your mind and so must have done some things right (or wrong) in the past to be part of your immediate recall memory. The percentage of people in the target audience that can remember the product or service in question is important, and one can often generalize that the organizations with the highest levels of unaided awareness normally have the highest share of market. While not always true, this is true much more often than not.

Within the category of unaided awareness, there is a measurement known as *first mention*, which is simply the percentage of people in the target audience that mention the name of your firm, your service, or your product first when asked for unaided recall of a particular group. Some marketing people feel that the first-mention percentage is even more important than the unaided level, as it indicates the place that the item occupies in the active memory.

In discussions of unaided awareness or first-mention levels with a group, one of the first questions is "what is a good percentage?" Unfortunately, there is no standard for this, as the important measurements are the relative levels of unaided (or first-mention) awareness of your organization and of the competition and the trend over time relative to this measurement. Absolute levels of unaided awareness also differ dramatically based on the target audience's interest in the category in question.

Aided awareness is at the other end of the spectrum. It consists of recognition of the entity when asked specifically whether one has heard of it (For example, "Have you ever heard of Clarion Marketing and Communications?" would be a question for which the answer would fall in the category of *aided awareness*). The percentage of positive (i.e., yes) responses is the measure of aided awareness of the entity for the target group being questioned.

In virtually every situation, the level of aided awareness is significantly greater than that of unaided awareness, often by a ratio of three or four to one. It is much more difficult to communicate to people in such a way that they will remember you immediately (without a prompt) than it is to give them a hint and then find out if they remember. Most organizations (or marketers) attribute far more importance to unaided awareness, both because of the greater difficulty of gaining unaided awareness and because, with aided awareness, one had no way of knowing whether the person questioned really recalls the entity in question or has simply chosen to agree (a phenomenon called yea-saying).

A third type of awareness is known as *recall*, defined as the ability to provide sufficient information to prove that awareness is real. If you are asked to name the leading management consulting firms in the United States, the names you mention at this stage become the unaided recall percentages. If you are asked next whether you are aware of company A, B, or C, you might indicate only C—this is the measure of aided awareness. If you are then asked to describe the services of company C, what you respond provides a first measure of recall. The level of this recall will often be a crucial factor determining how effective a communications program has been for an organization.

Some organizations, whether in consulting, banking, packaged goods or other services, work very hard to build unaided—or, at least, aided—awareness of their companies, but lose sight of the importance of generating specific recall regarding their various services. As a result, target customers are aware of the name but have no idea what the name represents. Clearly, this is not the optimal situation. The interrelationship between awareness and recall is particularly significant. If two firms have identical awareness levels (aided or unaided), but the target audience has significantly more true recall of the details of one organization, it is likely that the communications program for that company has been more effective.

There are basically two broad approaches generating awareness of your consulting practice. *Direct* methods represent efforts by your company to reach out to the target audience and deliver a specific message to them. Some of the most common of these will be the subject of this chapter. Chapter 8 will cover *indirect* methods of building awareness, which are more subtle and do not represent a frontal attack on the target audience. In neither chapter will the discussion differentiate between aided and unaided awareness. In general, the organizations that do the best job of implementing awareness-generating programs establish high levels of unaided awareness; others generate low levels of unaided awareness but might be successful in building aided awareness levels.

COLD-CALL LETTERS

A cold-call letter consists of a mailing sent to a prospective client whom you do not know or have no reason to believe has a need for the service you are offering. A mailing like this is normally carried out by purchasing a mailing list for the target audience and sending out a form letter, in which, frequently, the only tailored element is the name and title line and the salutation.

Some industries, such as life insurance companies, stock brokers, and realtors, rely on cold-call letters as their primary source of leads. These organizations learn to understand the way a cold-call program operates. It is a numbers game: For every thousand letters that go out, they know they will get a certain number of appointments, which will, in turn, produce a certain—smaller—number of sales. People starting new consulting companies often use cold-call letters; they generally believe strongly in their capabilities and the service they offer and feel that, if they just tell people about it, the telephones will ring off the hook. Unfortunately, this is rarely the case. Virtually everyone in business today receives a large volume of mail, and the probability of any of them following up a letter from a consultant trying to sell a service for which no need has been determined to exist is very remote. For a cold-call letter to have a chance of generating an appointment, the person who receives it must feel a need for the service outlined in the letter. In addition, chances are that a new company has not built any awareness among the target audience, and if awareness of a product or service does not exist, it is very difficult to get the attention of the target audience.

The obvious question at this point is, are there any advantages in using cold-call letters as part of a business-building plan for a new consulting organization? The answer is an unequivocal *yes*. As long as the person using the approach understands its limitations, cold-call letters have a definite place in a marketing program.

First of all, cold-call letters give the new consulting company a feeling of momentum. They represent a positive action to begin building the business. While the effort will produce minimal results, it is nonetheless a step toward establishing a client base.

However, for a program of this nature to have maximum effectiveness, the consultant must be committed to the following actions:

- Take the time to develop an effective mailing piece. Effective need not mean expensive or glitzy, but the piece must be capable of standing out among the clutter of mail that the target audience receives.

- Carefully think through the nature of the list that should be used for the mailing, as mailing to the wrong people would be a complete waste of time and money.

- Mail out only a limited number of letters each week, as it is essential to follow up each one with a telephone call to the person receiving the correspondence. Some people tend to implement mass mailings at one time, in the hope that this will set the telephone ringing immediately. These people apparently believe that more is always better, which I feel is absolutely incorrect for most consulting services soliciting business in this manner.

- Allocate a portion of every day to following up the letters that you mailed out the previous week. Further, you should try to make every follow-up call an opportunity to learn whether cold-call solicitations can work for your type of consulting service.

- Keep track of the most significant reasons the prospects give for not wanting to meet with you. Retain accurate records of the results of all calls that are made in order to help you to best classify the types of companies and the positions/functions within the companies that represent the most likely candidates for your service.

An important tip is to call prospects during those times of the day when they are more likely to pick up their own telephones—normally before 9:00 A.M. or after 4:45 P.M. Your chances of selling yourself to the prospect are much greater if you reach them directly. It is often virtually impossible to get through a secretary if you are not known to the prospect; you will find that the person you are contacting is always "in a meeting."

Second, cold-call solicitations represent a type of advertising and will help to build awareness of your service, although this is not the most efficient way to generate awareness (in terms of the costs per incremental person reached).

Thirdly, using the cold-call approach, you may be able to generate leads to other prospective clients that could be very effective. For example, on receiving an ambivalent response or a turn-down from the person contacted, the effective telephone solicitor will ask the individual for the names of other people in the organization or in some other company who might be viable prospects for the service offered. This is often the single most valuable part of any cold-call solicitation program.

Fourth, a cold-call mailing offers the consultant the opportunity to control the recipients by industry, function, or geographical region. Thus, you can choose to mail only to prospective clients in the part of the country where you are building your consulting practice.

Finally, a cold-call mailing can be relatively inexpensive or, at least, can fit into the budget you establish for the program. If you determine that you only have $2,500 to spend on this effort, you can tailor a program to meet this budget. Similarly, if you find that the effort is working and you want to add to the program, you can do so in virtually any increment.

The Cold-Call Letter—What It Should Contain

There is no standard formula for successful cold-call letters; the type of communication that works differ by prospective client type. However, the following represent some parameters that should be applicable to almost any situation.

The letter should be brief and to the point. The ideal letter should fit on one page, but it can be stretched to two. It is very unlikely that the reader will take the time to wade through a longer letter.

The letter should have a very arresting opening in order to get the attention of the reader. For example, if you are a consultant in the personnel relocation industry, you might open your letter with "Is your company tired of spending too much money or relocating employees? Our company can reduce the costs of employee relocation by x%."

The letter should have a succinct statement of the reason why. This is essentially a brief explanation of why or how your organization can deliver on the promise in the opening line in the letter. This is where you begin to establish some credibility; the individual reading the letter will make a determination as to whether the letter goes into the waste basket, deserves a follow-up call, or represents an interesting idea that will get a good reception when the individuals follows up the call.

The letter should have a great deal of white space. This means that it should be visually appealing to the reader, instead of looking as though it would be a chore to read. To achieve this, one need only to ensure that everything in the letter is necessary and expressed in the fewest possible words. If this is done, it should not be difficult to lay out a very appealing letter.

The letter should ask for an order (in this case, simply a follow-up call or letter from them) and provide a very easy way for the recipient to get in touch with you. Experience shows that if you do not ask for this, the chances of getting it are dramatically less. Then, if you give a telephone number, make sure that the phone is covered and available most of the time. Few things are more annoying than receiving a letter that is of interest and then being unable to connect with the person who sent the letter because the phone is either busy or unanswered.

Finally, the letter should tell the person that you will be contacting him or her to discuss an appropriate time for you to meet to discuss how your services might be of use. This is necessary; the individual should be expecting your call.

QUASI-COLD-CALL LETTERS

The difference between a quasi-cold-call letter and a cold-call letter is that a third party or event becomes an integral part of the solicitation.

Using networking can significantly improve the reception of the letter. For example, if you are seeking to get an appointment with the president of company X, your chances of getting through to him or her are much greater if your letter begins by saying that Joe Jones (who is someone the president knows well) suggested that you call, because . . . Networking is a very common practice in direct mail solicitation. Letters are far more likely to be read if the recipient sees a familiar name at the outset. Many of the third-party names could be generated during the follow-up of a cold-call campaign, while others might come from friends or relatives.

A second approach to a quasi-cold-call letter is to write to a person you met on an airplane, at a cocktail party, or in some other social situation. While the environment where you met the person probably was not right for talking business, it is not inappropriate to follow up with a letter mentioning the meeting and indicating that you would like to schedule an appointment when you could talk about how your consulting organization could be of assistance.

Another excellent way to solicit new business is to follow up an individual who has come into the public eye. For example, if the president of company X is quoted as saying that his or her company is going to make a major effort to reduce the costs of its retail store operation in the coming year, this could be an excellent opportunity for someone with consulting experience in this area to contact this individual. The letter would begin by commenting on the quote and then follow the same general format as that described above.

The ideal direct mail solicitation would involve only quasi-cold-communications as they are much more effective than cold communications. You should always be looking for ways to communicate to your prospects using a third-party endorsement. This will greatly increase their receptivity to the letters that you send.

ADVERTISING

One of the most common and most effective methods of building awareness is advertising. It is also the most risky. It can be very expensive, particularly if you wish to use it as a vehicle to generate high levels of top-of-mind awareness among your target audience group. Often it is one of the most difficult methods of building awareness to do correctly, because both creative and media considerations go into the development and implementation of every ad that is used. Advertising also can backfire if it is not on target or if the audience at which you are aiming the ads is not generally receptive to that type of business-building approach (as is very common among the medical profession, for example). And, if you make a mistake with an advertising program, it can take a long time and a lot of money to rectify it.

Media Options

The different types of media available to carry your advertising message are almost endless, and the only way to cover the alternatives is to discuss them in broad groups. Each industry will have its own unique media vehicles, which are often very important in terms of reaching prospective customers. One industry might be very tied into the key trade publication in the field, while another might be most responsive to advertising in trade show programs and at local industry conventions. The key is to understand the various media and the general advantages and disadvantages associated with each.

General business publications. This category includes newspapers such as the *Wall Street Journal, Barrons,* and the *Financial Times* and the business sections of major metropolitan area newspapers. It also includes general business magazines such as *Business Week, Forbes* or *Fortune.* Depending on the size of your practice (current or projected) and the size of the audience that you are seeking to reach, these can be excellent vehicles for delivering an advertising message. They all have a quality readership and reach a large number of executives in the business community. However, they also have some major disadvantages.

First, they are quite expensive in the absolute. For example, a one-quarter page ad in the national edition of the *Wall Street Journal* costs approximately $24,000, for only one insertion. Given that it is generally necessary to run an ad several times for it to have an impact (i.e., generate awareness), it is easy to see how very expensive a campaign in a major business paper can be.

Second, publications such as these reach a general business audience rather than a specific target group, so with each ad you waste a considerable percentage of the dollars employed through advertising to people who do not represent targets for your business.

Third, a small advertising campaign (whether in terms of ad size or number of times run) can get lost in one of these publications, since they carry a large amount of advertising, and much of it is from large companies with extensive budgets. The campaigns of these big organizations tend to dominate, and a small budget advertiser will have a difficult time getting enough reader attention to generate awareness.

Radio and television.   Often the first thing that comes to mind when one thinks of advertising is radio and TV, as these are the principal media that affect us in our daily lives. However, for a new consultant beginning a practice, the thought of using radio or television for advertising normally seems unrealistic to impossible. This is not always the case, though. Some radio and television opportunities might be available that could be affordable and very appropriate both in terms of the nature of the programming and the costs of the medium.

Radio advertising need be neither so expensive nor so general that it is inappropriate for your business. Today, much of the programming on AM radio is talk oriented and frequently offers programming designed to appeal to very selective advertisers and target audience segments. For example, one of the great radio stations in the United States is KABC, a talk radio station in Los Angeles that has been using this format for over 20 years. If you were to analyze the programming on this radio station, particularly on the weekends, you would find several different programs that could appeal to a consultant. If you are an architect or a landscape designer, a program on gardening or home repair might be very appropriate for advertising your practice. You might want to advertise on the Pamela Rose garden show, which airs on Sundays at 3 P.M. Or, if your consulting business relates to party planning, diet support, or catering, programs on foods and restaurants would be excellent vehicles for your advertising, and you might want to consider advertising on the Elmer Dills food and restaurant program which airs at 4 P.M. on Sundays or on the Merrill Shindler dining out program airing at 5 P.M. on Saturday. These represent only three examples of the unique programming options at only one radio station. There are hundreds of stations across the country that offer talk shows and other programs that could represent very appealing formats for an advertising message for your type of consulting business.

Television, too, need not be an impossible advertising option for your practice, particularly in light of the popularity of cable TV programming. If you were to consult the cable listings in your local area, you would find a wide variety of specialized programs. Business programs oriented toward both small business and the individual attract an audience that would probably be very receptive to a consulting practice in the financial planning, and investment area. Computer programs, which seek to provide everything from the basics of Lotus 1–2–3 to information about more sophisticated uses of personal computers, could be very appropriate media for the consultant with a practice oriented around providing computer services to individuals or businesses. Medical programming could offer an opportunity to consultants seeking to provide services to the medical community. Home improvement programs are good vehicles for architects or remodeling consultants. Advertising time on these types of programs can be purchased for a relatively small amount of money, with the absolute amount varying by cable area, depending on the size of the audience for each program.

The important thing to remember is that you should not automatically rule out television as a potential advertising medium, just because, on the surface, it seems to be too expensive. On the contrary, it might be less expensive than other options you are considering and might be much more effective.

Specific trade publications. One of the best media vehicles for your advertising is the trade publications that cover the industry or the function to which you are seeking to appeal. For example, if your consulting business is aimed at building revenues from the automotive industry, you will certainly want to consider advertising in *Automotive Trade News.* If you are seeking to develop a business in the soft drink, beer, or wine industry, you will want to look at *Beverage World* or *Beverage Industry Magazine.* Perhaps the focus of your consulting practice is more functional. If you are in the business of new product development for the consumer products industry, you might want to consider publications such as *Advertising Age* or *Ad Week* as possible journals to carry your ad. If you are in the business of providing pension consulting to small businesses, a publication such as *Pension Age* might be the ideal vehicle for you.

In net, trade publications can be excellent vehicles for your advertising, particularly if the industry to which you are directing the ads is receptive to this approach. These media can be highly specialized, both in terms of the industry and the people within the industry, and a specific publication may offer you a commercial environment tailored to your message.

The only obvious disadvantage of these media is their costs—the larger-circulation publications can be expensive—and the fact that trade publications often carry a great deal of advertising so there is a bigger chance that your ad will get lost among the others.

Yellow pages. Virtually every small business has been approached at one time or another by a Yellow Pages sales representative promoting the many benefits associated with placing an ad in this publication. It is my opinion, however, that very few types of consulting practices would benefit from Yellow Page advertising. This is not to suggest that it could not be effective for some practices, but, on balance, I do not recommend the Yellow Pages as an advertising vehicle. First, Yellow Pages' advertising is normally effective only when an individual is seeking to call someone in a particular field. For a person needing a plumber, a tire store, or a place to purchase costumes, the Yellow Pages can be an excellent tool. The individual simply goes to the Yellow Pages with a specific idea in mind and tries to find the right organization. These ads are not intended to build awareness but rather to attract attention at the time a call is being made. But, for a consulting practice, the purpose of advertising is to generate awareness, so that the other elements of the marketing mix (i.e., sales, pricing, promotion, etc.) will work more effectively.

Second, and very related to the above, most initial calls to a consulting business come as a result of referrals. It is very rare for someone to pull a name out of a general source like the Yellow Pages and call for services. The more professional the service sought, the less likely the use of the Yellow Pages to find it.

Third, the inquiries resulting from the Yellow Pages are likely to be of much lower quality than those from other sources. A person who uses the Yellow Pages as a resource for finding a consultant is not likely to be as strong a prospect as one who gets your name from a trade association, another consultant in a related field, or an industry contact aware of your services.

Fourth, ads in the Yellow Pages usually do not appear until at least one year after one makes the decision to use the vehicle. This is because of the annual printing cycle of most Yellow Page editions.

Fifth, there are often two or more different Yellow Page suppliers in any major market. If you make a decision to use this vehicle for advertising, then you must also decide which edition to use or whether to use all of them. This can result in extra expenses so that you can reach the full market effectively.

Sixth, because Yellow Pages are a very local medium and virtually every little town has its own edition, the mechanics of executing a meaningful Yellow Pages advertising program can be very complex, and the expense can build very quickly.

Despite all of the above, you should still evaluate the Yellow Pages as a potential option for advertising your practice. Yellow Pages do offer the advantage of localization, which permits advertising only in those editions that reach geographical areas of interest. For some types of consulting practices (i.e., landscape architecture, medicine, etc.), this localization could be very important; just be sure to evaluate the advantages and disadvantages of the Yellow Pages compared to other media.

Miscellaneous local media. A broad variety of other vehicles reach selective audiences. Just a few examples are advertising in programs for trade shows; advertising in community events such as golf tournaments, foot or bicycle races, fireworks displays, and so on; and sponsorship of hospitality suites, breakfasts, or coffee breaks at industry conventions.

All of these offer a unique opportunity to generate awareness of your practice. There are excellent reasons why and why not to get involved. Unfortunately, few good rules exist to make the decision quick and easy, as it will depend on a large variety of factors. However, if you evaluate each of the situations using the criteria discussed in the next section, the probability of a correct decision will be much greater.

Media Selection Guidelines

Advertising can be an extremely effective method to build awareness and generate leads *if* you select the correct media vehicle, use enough advertising weight to make an impression on the people you are trying to reach, and create strong advertising copy. This section will discuss several basic factors that will help determine what media are best to meet your specific needs. The next section will address how to develop advertising copy that will communicate your intended message.

How effectively will the media reach your target audience? This is clearly the most important consideration: If the publication or station you are considering does not appeal to the people to whom you are seeking to sell your services, then it is not worth using at any cost. Therefore, when considering the media vehicle, you should first establish the following:

- How many of your target audience prospects will be reached by the media? Virtually every media vehicle you consider should be able to give you an estimate of the reach based on your target audience definition.

- What is the composition of the media's audience with respect to your target audience? *Composition* refers to the percentage of the total audience that represents your target group. You will want to use media vehicles with the highest possible composition, as this will increase the relative efficiency of each dollar spent.

The overall effectiveness of the media is determined by the combination of total reach and composition. A media vehicle with a large total audience but low composition probably would not be nearly as good as one with a much smaller audience and a higher composition.

How efficiently will the media reach the target audience? Efficiency refers to the cost of using the media to reach target prospects, as compared to the cost of using another. Typically, these costs are expressed in terms of the CPM, or cost per thousand. For example, if we determine that a full-page ad in publication A costs $1000 and reaches 5000 target prospects, the CPM for the publication is $200 ($1000 divided by 5 units of 1000). The value of the CPM is that it provides an easy way to compare different media options with varied costs and audience sizes. For example, if you wanted to determine whether publication A was a more or less efficient media than magazine B, which has a cost of $9000 but reaches 65,000, you might first look at the comparative CPM—($200 for A compared to $138 for B).

What is the commercial and editorial environment? Some magazines or programs simply will be more conducive to the types of message you want to deliver, and this factor might outweigh the relative efficiency of the vehicle. Or you might prefer a publication because it has a much less cluttered commercial environment than does another, which might play an important part in your media selection decision. Many advertisers purposely select media vehicles that are more expensive on a CPM basis, just for the benefit of having a better environment for their ads.

What frequency is needed for the advertising to be effective? This is one of the most controversial of all issues in advertising. Unfortunately, there is very little hard data to support hard and fast rules for effective frequency levels. The best approach is to adhere to the following guidelines:

- Generally, it is better to run more ads in fewer vehicles than to run only a very few ads in many. This is because it takes time for an individual ad to register with the reader, a process referred to as frequency buildup.

- Most people favor running at least four print ads over a six-month period in a monthly publication or about six ads out of ten weeks in a weekly. The intent here is for the ad to be noticed with enough frequency that it will begin to generate some recognition/awareness.

- You should work hard to view your ad from the perspective of the target prospects, recognizing that it is only one of thousands that the prospective customer is exposed to in a given day. Therefore, it must be very easy to read and straightforward.

- It is normally better to run smaller ads more frequently than large ads less often. Specifically, I feel that two one-half page ads usually are better than one full-page ad, while four one-quarter page ads are better than two half-page ads. Naturally, this depends on the media vehicle used, the complexity of the message, and the effectiveness of the advertising copy.

What is the absolute media budget available? If you have a large budget to use for media, you can afford more media and/or more expensive vehicles. If your budget is small, the decisions regarding specific media vehicles, frequency of ads, and the size of the ads become much more difficult (and important).

Do your ads have a common look? If you are dealing with limited amounts of funds, you need to increase the impact of each advertising dollar spent. One of the techniques used most frequently is the adoption of a standard advertising format for every ad that you run. While the copy of the ad might change from publication to publication or from time to time, the overall look will not, so that everyone will recognize it as one of yours.

Another aspect of this technique is to run the ad in the same position in each publication. By keeping the position constant over time, you increase the chances that the reader will recognize your company.

Copy Considerations

One of the most difficult parts of any advertising program, whether it is for a consulting company, an auto dealership, or a laundry detergent, is the development of the advertising copy that will be used. Professional advertising copywriters are paid hundreds of thousands of dollars for their ideas and their skills in expressing them. As a start-up consultant, you probably will be your own copywriter, faced with the challenge of developing the most effective communication possible for your business.

Start with a strategy. As with all parts of the marketing mix, if you begin with a strategy that outlines what you want to achieve with your advertising, the probability of developing a successful campaign is greater.

1. Put together a very brief statement of what you want the advertising to accomplish. This should be realistic in scope and as specific as possible, an objective that can be achieved through advertising. Sometimes, people try to put a sales target into the advertising objective, without realizing that this is not a realistic goal for advertising (alone).

2. Identify the reason why someone reading the ad should call on you. This should be as brief and specific as possible, stated in such a way that it will be clearly understood by all prospective clients.

3. Identify the most important copy points that you wish to register in the ad, focusing on as few as possible, in order to retain the emphasis on the key areas.

4. Provide a brief description of the tone you wish to have in the advertising. For example, are you seeking to develop advertising that will be very serious, or will it contain humor? Will it appear to be somewhat snobby, or will it have general appeal? These are the types of considerations that should go into this decision.

Respect the value of the headline when using print advertising. The most important part of any print advertisement is the headline. Over 70 percent of all people exposed to a print ad read the headline *only*. Therefore, you need to have a headline that is memorable, relevant to your business, and of sufficient interest to motivate a large percentage of readers to read further.

Incorporate your name into the ad in many places. Whether you are working with print or broadcast advertising, frequent and obvious name mentions are essential, as they will dramatically increase the probability of achieving recall.

Be single-minded in the ad focus. One of the biggest mistakes people make when creating advertising is trying to accomplish too much in the ad; they end up writing something that is so complex that no message is delivered. The best ads have only one main idea, and the copy is focused on delivering that concept to the reader.

Make the ad appealing to read. This seems very obvious, but if you look at the advertisements in a typical trade journal, you will see why I include it as a basic guiding principle. Your ad(s) should encourage the reader to read the body of the copy, either by a combination of clever headlines and subheads and/or by an effective use of white space to make the ad seem accessible and easy to read.

Break through the clutter. This is essential, particularly with small-space or small-budget advertising. The key is to use some technique, perhaps in the graphics of the ad or the headline, to make your ad stand out from the mass of others. This is very important; if the ad does not stand out, it probably will never be read.

Use the language of the target audience. Whenever you write an ad for your business, it is vital that the language you use be understood by the people who are reading the ad. We often tend to get very involved with the jargon of our particular industry and just assume that others will understand it as well. Unfortunately, this is not normally the case, and it is very important to make an extra effort to talk to the audience in a language that is familiar.

Consultants' Advertising—a Specific Example

The following specific example will illustrate how a consulting organization can use advertising effectively.

A major focus of our consulting practice in 1987 was servicing the financial services industry in the areas of marketing, sales, and promotion issues. After October 19th, the day of the stock market crash, our financial services consulting business eroded quickly, as banks and other financial services organizations determined that they would need to cut costs drastically because of the problems with the overall economy.

We were aware that many (if not most) financial service organizations were very confused about what to do with their marketing programs at this time, in light of all the excitement and general chaos created by the crash. Because of this environment, we decided it might be advantageous to mount a brief but highly targeted advertising campaign to see if it would result in additional leads.

The result was the advertisement shown in Figure 7.1 on page 108 which ran six times in *American Banker*, a trade publication selected because of its excellent reach among senior executives in financial institutions.

Several of the key features of this ad reinforce some of the principles discussed earlier.

- The headline was intended to break through the clutter and get to the target audience in a meaningful way. In light of the situation that existed in the postcrash environment, we felt that "Help!"was one concept to which most bank executives would respond.

Figure 7.1 An Example of a Highly Successful Advertisement for Consulting Services

- The body copy under the headline was intended to get right to the point, tying in the current environment and the need for help that we perceived among bank executives. The copy was written intentionally to be very brief and to make the point that we understood bank executives' needs and that our expertise could help them.

- The ad also offered excellent name identification, accomplished by putting our name in reverse type, so it would stand out and be noticed.

- The ad also named a specific person to contact and gave a telephone number to call for information.

The results of this very brief (and inexpensive) campaign were extremely positive. We signed thousands of dollars of new consulting business and made contacts with other organizations that did not buy then but became clients in the future. We had identified a unique situation for a campaign, had developed a single-minded ad that talked to the need of the target audience, and had followed the principles of good advertising by creating an ad that would break through all the clutter in the newspaper.

DIRECT-MARKETING ACTIVITIES

Another option in the arsenal of tools that can help build awareness of your organization is the use of direct marketing. Essentially, direct marketing is an extension of the cold-call and quasi-cold-call communications method discussed earlier in this chapter. The principal difference lies in the content of the mailing piece used in the direct-marketing activities. For example, cold-call mailings generally include only a broadcast letter, whereas direct marketing typically involves also sending something extra as well.

There are several very important reasons why a consultant might want to use direct marketing to generate awareness of the new organization and to source leads. The main objective is to break through the clutter. Most business people receive hundreds of pieces of mail each week, most of which falls into the category of junk mail and is thrown away. The purpose of a direct-mail program is to make such a inviting presentation to the target customers that they will read and remember the piece. Another objective is to send a message to the prospect. This message might have to do with the nature of the consultant's business, the way the consultant can operate (e.g., a demonstration of creativity), or the types of services that the company offers. Finally, many direct-marketing programs can be very memorable and therefore help to build unaided (top-of-mind) awareness of the company. Further, if the communication is particularly creative or unusual, it might also help build awareness by virtue of the word of mouth communications that will be started by the recipient.

Items that Can Be Included in a Direct-Mail Package

The following will provide some examples of items that have been used effectively by consulting and service organizations in direct-mail programs.

Newsletters. One very effective method of direct mail for a consulting organization is to create a newsletter about the happenings in your industry and send it to the target audience. For example, a marketing consultant I know was seeking to establish a new practice in a high technology field. He began by conducting a market research study of product ownership in the industry, summarizing highlights from that study, and using them as the basis for a newsletter. The objective of the newsletter was to communicate to the target audience that this new consulting company was knowledgeable about the industry, the reason why being the hard data provided. The newsletter was also intended to interest the recipients in having more information about some of the topics that it mentioned, in the hope of turning up some excellent leads that could be turned into new clients.

While newsletters can be a very effective way to build awareness and to generate quality leads, they have some very significant problems of which you should be aware. Specifically, it can be expensive to develop a quality newsletter. Whether the work consists of implementing a marketing research study or simply gathering meaningful secondary source data germane to your ares of expertise, it takes time and money. And many new consultants have plenty of time but virtually no money. Further, using a newsletter for promotional purposes requires you to adhere to a production schedule. A newsletter must be published with some regularity to have a meaningful impact, and such publication, even if only four times a year, can be a big burden, particularly when your consulting practice begins to get very busy. Finally, the quality of the newsletter must be consistently excellent. This requires you to identify meaningful topics to cover in each issue and to ensure that they are written in a professional manner that is consistent with the image of the organization.

Samples of your product. Many types of consulting practices can develop direct-marketing packages that provide recipients with examples of their work or, at least, their approach to consulting assignments. Samples of a consulting product might include the following:

- A company operating in the computer software business can (and frequently does) send out a demo disk to prospective clients. This gives prospects an opportunity to try out the program on a very small scale. If they like the demo, they can order the regular disk or the software consulting service that is being promoted.

- A consulting company that services clients in any phase of graphic design can easily send samples (photographs) of their work to prospective clients. If the company also includes a cover letter indicating why the examples are good and how the talent they represent can be effective for the prospect, the odds of generating interest in the service are particularly good. Peterson & Blyth, the New York City graphics design firm mentioned in Chapter 5, does an excellent job of mailing prospects copies of its latest package design successes. This maintains prospects' top-of-mind awareness of the firm, and probably is a very important part of Peterson & Blyth's success.

- A consultant that operates in the sales promotion, contesting, or brochure production business also can easily send samples of his or her work to prospective clients. In the case of these businesses, it is often possible (and normally very desirable) to send actual samples of work.

- A strategic consultant who does not really have a product to show for his or her work can send prospective clients copies of articles that he or she has written. These can be very effective, but they must have been published to have meaningful impact. White papers and position pieces can be very scholarly and often very thought provoking but, in most cases, they simply do not have the effect of an article that has been published in a well-recognized industry publication. Even so, the content of the article is more important than the publication that carried it. The material must be excellent and very representative of the type of thinking that the consulting organization offers. Copies of newspaper or magazine stories that have been written about the consultant or his or her company also can send effective third-party endorsement to prospects.

Novelty direct-mail pieces.   These are items that have been created especially for a direct mailing and are intended to send a particular message to the prospect. For example, a consulting company called Blue Chip sent prospects a box printed with the message "we can show you how to lick your problem." When prospects opened the box, they saw a series of lollipops that spelled out the word *problem.* This item got the immediate attention of the recipient and was very effective in motivating the recipient to read the inside copy that told how the consulting organization was going to help solve the problem.

Another organization used a credit-card-sized device that theoretically measured stress when the recipient pressed the "magic" spot on the card. While this device probably did not really measure stress, it did get the attention of the recipient and, importantly, enabled the organization to inform the recipient of some action that would reduce the amount of stress that the individual experienced.

Finally, another firm used a very short pair of scissors to communicate that it could show prospects how to short cut some problems and come to a solution more effectively and efficiently.

SUMMARY

Direct methods of awareness building represent one option that you can use to generate leads for your consulting practice. They can be very effective if used properly but, at the same time, can become extremely expensive and time-consuming if they are used haphazardly. Still, although they generally are not the most cost-effective way to create leads, when you need to generate some revenues, the direct methods of awareness building are the quickest way to make things happen.

8 Building Awareness of Your Business— Indirect Methods

The indirect methods of awareness building normally do not involve an out-of-pocket expenditure, take longer to generate new business, and usually cannot be planned with the same degree of precision as can the direct methods. In my opinion, both the direct and indirect methods of building awareness are important to the growth of a consulting business, but, if it were necessary to eliminate one from a marketing plan, I would recommend that the direct methods go first. Most consulting organizations, however, tend to do some of the direct methods and very few of the indirect. This is because of the time commitment that is often required to execute the indirect programs and the longer payback period associated with the indirect approach. Still, if you pursue one of the activities described in this chapter, you may find that the long-term benefits amply reward your patience.

GET INVOLVED IN COMMUNITY ACTIVITIES

One very effective way to build awareness of your practice and, therefore, to generate leads involves participating in local community activities, such as the Boy Scouts, the local PTA, your church or synagogue, the

United Way, or any of the hundreds of similar organizations that are always seeking volunteers.

If you choose to follow this approach, consider the following guidelines:

- Only get involved in causes to which you have a personal commitment. It is very important that you enjoy participating in the organization; otherwise, your work on its behalf (and, ultimately, for the benefit of your practice) will not be effective.

- Aspire to a leadership position in the organization, so you have excellent visibility and contacts within the group. A consultant who is basically a joiner will not have nearly the effectiveness as will a person who becomes a leader.

- When you get involved in projects in the organization, try to work in areas that relate as closely as possible to your professional life. This will give you an opportunity to demonstrate your skills in the area.

- Keep a low profile in the organization about the nature of your consulting practice. It is always much better for someone to inquire about the type of business you operate than for you to push that information yourself. Many consultants make themselves quite unpopular by too obviously using community organizations to generate awareness and leads.

- When you are assigned a task in the organization, do it well, cheerfully, and punctually. This will impress those in the group whom you would ultimately like to have as clients.

- Work hard to get assigned to projects that are optimal for you—assignments that are very visible, in your basic professional discipline (to ensure you perform well), and of particular interest to the leadership of the organization.

GET ARTICLES PUBLISHED

In my opinion, this is one of the most important things you can do to build awareness (and a reputation) for your practice. By writing an article under your own byline for a newspaper or magazine, you will gain useful exposure, because of the numbers of people who read the publication and see your name (and, hopefully, a company description) in the biographical sketch. You will also build credibility in your area of expertise, especially if your article is published by a key industry magazine or newspaper. Finally, you can use reprints of the article for merchandising, giving out (or mailing) copies to people who did not see it originally.

The key to this method of awareness building is to write good articles that attract reader attention, demonstrate your professional skills, and leave the reader with some valuable insights. Also, in my experience, effective placement of articles for publication can be a very valuable element of the marketing program for a new consulting practice. I can attribute several hundred thousand dollars of consulting revenues that I have generated to the placement of articles in the right publications. It is essential that you place your material with great caution. A terrific article in a meaningless publication will not do you nearly as much good as the same article placed in a leading industry journal.

WRITE A BOOK!

While this clearly is much easier said than done, there is no denying the benefits that you can derive by publishing a book on your topic. The world anoints you with instant credibility, which will open many doors. If you develop an effective plan of attack, you can easily merchandise the publication of your book to benefit your consulting practice.

GET ON TELEVISION OR RADIO

This suggestion always raises the eyebrows of many students. They always view television as the forbidden medium for promoting a product or service, because of the difficulty (which often seems more like an impossibility) of getting on the air. However, if you remain alert to the opportunities, you quickly should discover that there are some very significant television and radio shows that would be perfect for you. Further, and of significant importance, it is not impossible to get on these shows.

A personal example might be helpful here. One morning, I was riding my exercise bicycle, watching the morning news on CBS, when a program came on called "Business This Morning." This program highlights the major business news of the previous day and the stories that are anticipated to be in the news during the coming day. A daily segment of this program is "Business Focus," which covers feature business news stories of many different varieties that would be of interest to the viewers. While watching this program, it occurred to me that I might be able to get on the show because of the book I recently had published on focus group research. It seemed like a real long shot, but I decided to write to the program to inquire about this possibility.

In less than four weeks, we filmed a two-and-one-half-minute segment on focus group research that aired on both CBS and the Financial News Network, giving me and my company excellent exposure to a national audience. Purchasing this time would have required hundreds of thousands of dollars, but we got it free. The key was the letter we sent, which contained a convincing story of why the program should cover the topic of focus groups and how my presence on the program could be the best way to achieve this coverage. (We also taped the program to use in speeches and presentations whenever we are selling focus group research services to prospective clients.)

The lesson here is to be always on the lookout for opportunities to gain free air time on television or radio to promote your consulting service. Identify target programs that would be ideal for you, in terms of the audience they reach, and provide them with a rationale for why they should put you on their program. Most of the programs on radio and television that would appeal to you are always on the lookout for strong programming; you just have to develop a story and sell it to them.

TEACH YOUR SUBJECT AT A UNIVERSITY

Most colleges and universities employ adjunct professors to teach part-time on evenings or weekends. If you can obtain a position to teach your area of expertise at the university, you will get exposure to all the students who take your course. In many cases, these students work part-time or full-time, which is why they are going to school on evenings or weekends. Each one represents a potential client lead for you, as they all will see you as the expert in this area and therefore may recommend you to their company.

Teaching at a university or college also offers you the opportunity to promote yourself in the local newspapers. The fact that you are teaching this subject on a part-time basis at College A is news to your local paper and, probably, to the paper in the college town as well. Both would likely be inclined to carry articles about this position. I know that the newspaper coverage I have received because of the teaching I have done has generated many tens of thousands of dollars in consulting revenues.

Finally, teaching your subject in a university setting is an impressive résumé builder that will increase your overall worth to prospective clients.

PARTICIPATE IN TRADE MEETINGS AND SHOWS

An excellent way to build awareness for your consulting practice is to become involved in a significant way in target industry trade shows and meetings. The best approach is to give a presentation on a topic about which you are an expert. You and your company get direct exposure to the groups of people who come to hear your session, where you have the chance to demonstrate the capabilities that you offer in your consulting practice. You also get excellent exposure simply by virtue of being on the program. Many people who do not go to the convention or even those who go to the convention but not to your presentation will see your name (and that of your company) in the program. Furthermore, as a speaker at a convention, you usually will be provided with a special type of badge that will distinguish you from the other consultants who are present. This badge generates special attention for you and thus helps to build awareness of you and your company.

Another option is to have an exhibit at the convention, which might be very beneficial for you. First, it will give you excellent exposure, as most of the people who attend industry conventions spend significant time visiting the various exhibits. Second, it gives you the opportunity to meet some very targeted prospects that could become clients over time.

Third, depending on the nature of your consulting practice, an exhibit in the convention hall might give you the chance to demonstrate to prospective clients what you do. For example, if your business relies heavily on computer software, you can demonstrate this at the convention. Indeed, if your practice deals with any type of tangible product or one that can be made tangible via such things as photos or video tape, the convention exhibit could be an excellent vehicle for you.

There are, however, some definite disadvantages to taking an exhibit in a convention hall. As an exhibitor, you are classified as a vendor, which, to many consultants, is very derogatory, since they view themselves as professionals, rather than as peddlers of services. The image associated with consulting companies that show their wares in a convention exhibit hall may not be consistent with what you are trying to achieve with your company positioning.

It is also very difficult to spend meaningful time with people who come by your booth to see what services you offer. You are forced to spend only a few minutes with each person who stops by, and that time may be so superficial that it does not serve your best interests.

By exhibiting at a convention, moreover, you give your competitors the opportunity to learn a great deal about your company, in terms of the services you offer and the way you price them. Depending on the nature of your business, this can work to your disadvantage, as the competition will be able to position their services more effectively against you.

Participating on a panel discussion is another way to take part in a convention. While this is not as effective as being a key speaker, it is far better than having no special place in the meeting. As a panel member, you do hold a special position among the people attending the sessions in which you are involved, and you have the chance to demonstrate your skills when you are called on to answer questions. You also benefit from the exposure you likely will get in the convention brochure and you will derive some additional benefits from the fact that the badge you wear during the convention will normally be different from that of others, thus drawing attention to you and your company.

The least effective way to generate awareness for your company at a convention is simply to attend without having any special role. While this is better than not going to the meeting at all, it will not do a great deal to build awareness for your company. You will be just one of many people wandering around the hall, and the only people who become aware of you will be those who you meet during the sessions. Eventually, even this type of involvement could be helpful to you in building your consulting practice, as you will get to know people in the industry, but this takes a great deal of time, and it is always better to have some special role in the meeting.

TAKE AN ACTIVE ROLE IN KEY INDUSTRY TRADE ASSOCIATIONS

Most industry associations are very interested in having people participate on committees and/or in the management of their organizations. For the consultant who is seeking visibility for his or her organization, a key role in an important industry trade association can be an excellent way to gain exposure to client prospects. Further, if the consultant attains the right position in the organization, he or she may gain excellent awareness for his or her company.

While the assumption of a leadership role in an industry trade association represents a somewhat longer-term approach to building awareness than do some of the other approaches that have been recommended, this course usually is very worthwhile to pursue. And simply becoming involved in some of the committees of the trade association will bring immediate benefits, if only from the contacts made within the organization.

GIVE SEMINARS ON TOPICS THAT RELATE DIRECTLY TO YOUR CONSULTING PRACTICE

Seminars on topics of interest to your target clients can be offered in any of the following formats:

- Free standing, simply on an open invitation basis to people you choose to invite either via direct mail or by some other method of communication

- As part of another meeting, such as a trade convention, a client retreat, or the like

- At a college or university as a special course of limited duration

MAINTAIN AN ACTIVE NETWORK

One of the very best ways to generate high levels of top-of-mind awareness for your consulting practice is to work hard to develop a network of prospects and then to stay in contact with them. Use the telephone effectively; some consultants allocate time every day for calling people just to stay in touch. Also, take advantage of appropriate socializing opportunities. During a given week or month, you may have many chances to use a lunch, dinner, or evening to build awareness for your company. Many consultants try never to eat lunch alone, using that time to meet with prospective clients or other key people who might become referral sources. Other people make a point of attending major social activities in their industry or their town so that they can maintain a high profile.

One of the most difficult problems many consultants have with the networking approach is finding reasons to stay in touch with the prospect universe. If you take an organized approach to this objective, it will be much easier for you to find good excuses to make contact.

Some consultants keep track of the birthdays of their clients and prospects and always call or write to them on their birthdays. This type of communication usually is very well received and certainly helps to maintain high levels of awareness for your organization.

A second approach that has been used very effectively by many people involves the establishment of an index file of the special interests of the people in your network universe. Say that, during the course of a meeting with a prospect, you noticed that he collects antique music boxes. You would note this information on a special card and file it in your interest file. Then, when you read an article in a magazine that refers to antique music boxes, you cut the piece out and send it to the interested party, with a brief note indicating you thought he would be interested in seeing the article. When the person receives the article and the note, he will be very favorably impressed, both because you remembered that he was interested in this area and because you took the time and trouble to send the article to him. For this individual, you will have a high level of top-of-mind awareness.

One of the best ways to maintain an active level of awareness among a large group of high-potential prospects is to write to people when special announcements are printed about them. I make it a point to congratulate friends, colleagues, and prospects whenever I read about them in the papers, whether the announcement has to do with a promotion, a marriage, or a new position in another company. I find it very rewarding to stay in touch with people that way, and the persons receiving the letters certainly appreciate the fact that someone has taken the time to write.

Another excellent reason to write to someone (or to call them) is to pass along greetings from a common friend or to touch base after a long silence as a result of a meeting with a common friend. For example, if the name of an old college friend came up during a conversation with someone with whom you and the other individual were friendly in the past, it would not be inappropriate to send a note to the "lost" person, mentioning that you and your common friend were thinking about her. Or perhaps you had a meeting with a stranger and discover that you have a close mutual friend. This would be a fine opportunity to write or call the other individual to communicate how you met your common friend.

Develop a Vehicle for Network Contact

The process of building and, importantly, maintaining a network can be very difficult. The task requires regular attention, and, when business is particularly good, it is sometimes very difficult to take the time away from revenue-generating activities to work on keeping up with the network. While telephone and socializing, mentioned earlier, may do the trick, a few more formal approaches can also be useful to the enterprising consultant. These specialized vehicles can help you to build and maintain a network of highly targeted persons, while, at the same time, build high levels of awareness for you and your company.

Develop an alumni association. A few major companies have spawned many of today's leaders in various fields. One would not have to think long to come up with organizations such as Procter & Gamble in consumer goods marketing, A.C. Nielsen in survey research, IBM in computers, and AT&T in telecommunications. If you operate a consulting business that seeks to develop contacts with people from a common background, a place to begin is the organization where they got their basic training. For example, currently there exists a Procter & Gamble Alumni Association, made up of personnel who have been at P&G in some advertising/marketing/brand management capacity. This alumni association actually has an annual meeting each year (for the express purpose of networking) and, importantly, maintains an alumni directory, which is updated each year with the current business and home addresses of the various people. New people also are added to the directory during the year.

This directory was created by a very innovative individual in the executive search business. His theory was that by creating the alumni association, and maintaining the directory, he would become the main authority on people who have been at P&G. Since these people are prime candidates for many marketing jobs, their whereabouts is of great interest to personnel executives in U.S. businesses. If an organization wished to hire someone with a P&G marketing background, it could go to the directory and try to handle it directly or, more than likely, contact John Thomas, the author and father of the P&G alumni association. In other words, through the director, Mr. Thomas built a level of awareness for himself in the executive search business and, at the same time, has been able to maintain an extensive network of people that he can use for recruiting or approach as potential clients for search assignments.

Develop and edit an industry newsletter. The type of newsletter discussed earlier in the chapter was oriented toward communicating to a target audience the technical skills you have, as a way to interest them in contacting you for consulting assignments. The newsletter concept I am discussing here is oriented toward collecting and disseminating personnel-related information about the people in a particular industry. For example, a consultant operating in the market research industry might want to consider establishing a network newsletter for corporate marketing research persons that tells them about job openings in the industry and major personnel changes within the client side of the industry (i.e., promotions, job changes, marriages, new children, etc.). Such a publication would very likely get high levels of readership among a broad group of target customers, including corporate marketing research personnel, corporate personnel executives seeking to fill positions, corporate marketing personnel thinking about going into marketing research, and executive recruiters looking to announce their openings in the newsletter. Moreover, this newsletter would establish the consultant as the focal point for a great deal of very important information and build contacts and inside relationships with a great number of people. If these relationships are handled effectively, they can be nurtured into new clients for the consulting business.

Hold a symposium. A third method for building a very meaningful network of potential clients is to give a symposium in your industry on a topic that will have a broad appeal among the target audience. This option, however, is not recommended for the very new consultant, because it might represent too much of a financial risk and too great a workload for someone just starting out in business. However, for the consulting organization that has been in business for some time and has a reasonable financial backing, this type of networking program could be very effective.

Organizing a symposium program involves the following steps:

1. Develop a program for the symposium, based on very important issues in the industry that will generate immediate attention from the target audience. The agenda should cover the entire length of the symposium which, if it is your first, probably should be no longer than one full day.

2. Draw up a target audience list, indicating who will be invited to attend the program.

3. Determine the financial and operating parameters of the symposium. For example, will attending the conference involve only a day trip, or will it require some (or all) of the people to stay overnight? If they need to stay overnight, will you provide accommodations or leave that up to them? You must also consider the costs of serving meals and renting a facility in order to calculate the expense of the entire effort. You will quickly learn that this is a very costly way to generate leads; normally, though, the quality of the leads is excellent.

4. Design a high-quality invitation that will capture the attention of the recipients and communicate to them the nature of the meeting and the importance of the contact. Depending on when the program is scheduled to happen (i.e., in the evening, on a weekend, or during the week; locally or at a distant place), the level of interest among the recipients will vary.

5. Incorporate a response vehicle into the invitations so that you can keep close track of the responses. In addition, it would be very desirable for you personally to invite key people.

If you are successful in generating enough interest to justify holding the event, then it is essential that you follow through on all the operational details to ensure that the meeting is as professional as possible. This meeting will reflect on you; if you spend the time and the money to hold it, you must get as much as possible out of it.

Leverage public relations opportunities.   Many people in the consulting business feel that public relations are the key to building awareness and that almost everything you do should give you the opportunity to secure public relations coverage.

Seek publicity for any speeches that you give to industry organizations. Take the time to develop public relations releases about these speeches. These releases should be sent to any publications that might have some interest in you or the topics about which you are speaking. Most local newspapers will carry stories about residents or people who work in their town.

As I said earlier, articles in my local town newspaper have generated tens of thousands of dollars in consulting revenues. In addition, most industry trade publications will carry well-written public relations releases.

Attempt to secure public relations coverage for any important activities that occur in your organization—your opening, a move to larger quarters, the addition of personnel to your staff, awards you have won, and so on. While none of these will do wonders for you individually, all have news value and each will contribute a little bit to building awareness for your company.

Obtain public relations coverage for other things you or your employees do. For example, when this book is published, I will mount a significant public relations campaign in a variety of different media, for the express purpose of promoting my company. This publicity also will help to sell the book and to generate new clients for my basic consulting business. Similarly, if you take a major position in a local, regional, or national organization, whether community- or industry-related, you should try to get as much press coverage as possible, including in the release information about your company and the services it offers.

Volunteer your services to the media as a source of information about a particular industry or functional specialty area. Most newspapers and magazines (particularly trade publications) retain a list of experts they can contact for information on specific topics. They use these people as sources of both information and of quotes for their articles. To become a resource for a publication, write a letter to the editor (or a specific columnist) indicating your areas of expertise and willingness to be a resource and quotable source for them.

SUMMARY

The indirect methods of building awareness are often the most effective, but they require an ongoing commitment to this type of activity. Because you do not have control over the exposure that is received, as is the case with the direct methods, it is necessary to keep up the pressure for this approach to work. This means that you must carefully select the best organizations in which to become involved, commit to a regular schedule of publishing articles in key trade journals, and choose the right trade organizations in which to involve yourself and your people.

The payoff from indirect methods is slower than with the direct approach to building awareness; however, if you are willing to spend the time, the awareness will grow and the business leads will come.

9 Developing a Brochure

For the purposes of this chapter, a brochure is a printed document of virtually any length or format that provides an overview of the capabilities of a consultant or a consulting organization, in order to help a prospective client make a positive purchase decision. The key is that it is a more formalized, printed document, not simply a typewritten page or two summarizing the scope of the business. This is not to suggest that you could not develop a brochure using one of today's many desktop printing processes. In fact, creating that type of brochure normally does not involve a meaningful financial decision, as would the development of a more formalized document. However, the same principles regarding content development apply to both types of brochure.

This chapter will discuss the brochure from both a strategic and an operational perspective. It will raise issues that you may not want to face, such as whether you really need a brochure and what role the brochure actually plays in the overall marketing effort of your consulting practice. It is also intended to provide hands-on assistance that will help you develop the best possible brochure for your business, in light of the budgetary constraints that you undoubtedly face. By the end of this chapter, you should be in a position to determine the role of the brochure (if any) in your overall marketing effort.

THE ROLE OF THE BROCHURE IN THE MARKETING MIX

In my opinion, the brochure is probably the element of the marketing mix that is most overrated by new consultants. Dozens (if not hundreds) of very successful consulting practices do not even have a brochure; hundreds (if not thousands) have developed very comprehensive and/or fancy brochures but are struggling to survive. Yet, one of the first things that some people do when they make the decision to enter the consulting business is to develop a brochure. Indeed, many students have taken my course at Harvard for the principal purpose of learning how to write their brochures. The unfortunate thing is that these people often feel that the brochure is the key to their marketing effort, and it becomes the focal point of their activities during the initial few weeks or months of their businesses. Further, many people simply execute something very quickly so that they have a document, as though the mere existence of a brochure will create leads for them. In most cases, they never think through some of the most basic issues of the business that relate to the brochure, such as:

- What is the purpose of the brochure?

- To whom is the brochure directed?

- What are the most important points that the consultant wishes to make in the brochure?

- What should be the look of the brochure and the tone and manner of the document?

- How will the brochure be used in the consulting practice?

Because of this lack of strategic orientation in the brochure development process, it is quite predictable that most people are very unhappy with their first brochures. With almost frenzied looks they tell me at the beginning of class that they must do something with their brochures, blaming them for their businesses' disappointing starts. Typically, they have spent a lot of time working on their brochures, focusing on each word to ensure that it is what they want. But I have yet to meet a student who comes to the class with a brochure strategy and indicates that the problem is how to develop a document that is consistent with the goals of the strategy.

The first decision that you should make is whether you even need to have a brochure for your business. This decision will normally depend on the following factors:

1. *What are the industry standards among the competition?* If all the consultants with whom you will be competing have brochures, it is likely that you will need one too. The key decision then relates to the format that you require; this will be covered later in this chapter.

2. *What prospects expect.* Some client organizations expect you to have a brochure, much the way they expect you to have a business card. To sell your services to these prospects, you will need to have a brochure, and, once again, the key decision concerns the format of the document.

3. *How you anticipate marketing your consulting service.* Assessing the need for a brochure depends crucially on how it will be used. As one would expect, if the consultant feels that direct mail or convention participation will be a very important part of the marketing plan, the need for a brochure will be much greater than if most of the marketing/selling will occur on a personal basis.

4. *How much time you can spend developing the brochure.* While most people establishing a consulting business generally have a great deal of time available in the beginning, some people begin their practices with clients and lots of work; for them to spend time working on a brochure might not be in their best overall interest.

5. *What funds you can allocate to a brochure.* This is often the area that determines the format of the brochure, rather than whether or not one is needed. If you determine that a brochure is needed, the approach will normally be to develop one immediately within the existing budget, rather than to hold off until more money is available.

In evaluating whether your consulting practice needs a brochure, you will probably find it very helpful to understand the rationales of others who have faced the same decision. Those that do not have a brochure often indicate that they simply cannot develop a written description of their services that makes them happy; therefore, they avoid the issue by not having a brochure. This is frequently the case when a consulting practice is poorly defined. Others feel that developing a brochure constitutes a needless expense and is also far too time-consuming. Some want to have flexibility about what they tell prospective clients about the nature and scope of their services. Consultants who have not determined the degree of specialization they wish to pursue in their practices want to stay reasonably general in the scope of their services, in the hope that this will generate greater overall revenues. For them, a brochure becomes more of a hindrance than a help. Still others do not develop a brochure because of the transitional nature of their businesses, either in terms of people or of the scope of the practice. For example, consultants in a growth phase of the business, where they are adding people and services at a fast pace, might want to wait until the practice solidifies before they try to develop a formal brochure. Finally, some consultants feel they simply do not need a brochure, because their own reputations and past experiences are much more persuasive than any brochure could be. Therefore, for them the brochure would be superfluous.

Many consultants that do have a brochure find that it is a valuable sales tool, both for personal selling of their services and for responding to inquiries about their capabilities. To these people, the brochure obviates the need to develop a detailed letter each time someone asks for an overview of their services. Some use the brochure as a leave-behind at the conclusion of a new business presentation, to serve as a reminder of the information that has been communicated during the meeting. These people feel that providing prospects with something formal, permanent, and printed adds professionalism to their overall approach. Finally, some new consultants use brochures very effectively to attract people to their organizations. Many owners of small consulting companies have told me a printed brochure gives job applicants a feeling of stability and provides a much better first impression than if no such document is available.

PRINTED VERSUS DESKTOP BROCHURE DEVELOPMENT

One of the first questions that most new consultants ask when considering the brochure issue is whether they should formalize the brochure to the extent of having it printed or start with a very informal alternative, such as a collection of typed pages or a computer-generated brochure produced with one of the many desktop publishing packages. This decision needs to be made early in the process, as it will determine the magnitude of the entire brochure development effort. My experience in the consulting business and discussions with new consultants that have taken my course have led me to think that the following factors will have the greatest effect on this decision:

1. *Budget availability.* If funds are very tight during the start-up phase of a business, most people will decide to begin with a very informal brochure, using the money that would have gone into a printed version for operational and living expenses.

2. *Image.* The degree to which your image is important to you will also significantly affect your decision as to the kind of brochure you will produce. If the image of your organization is particularly important to you or your prospects, you must have a printed brochure. If image is not particularly important, a less formal version should be satisfactory.

3. *Permanence.* Often during the early days of a consulting business, the organization is in a state of flux, and the owner (or group) is determining the manpower, the roles and responsibilities of people, and the specific services that will be offered. If these issues are not firmly established, it makes little sense to develop a permanent brochure.

4. *Time.* To develop a formal, printed brochure can take several weeks (if not months), and many new consultants do not plan the beginning of their practices with much advance notice. For this reason, they often decide to begin with a typed brochure and then follow up with a printed version several weeks or months later.

INTERNAL VERSUS EXTERNAL BROCHURE DEVELOPMENT

The decision has been made that you will develop a brochure for your consulting practice. You must now make a second very important decision before you can proceed effectively: What process will you use to develop your brochure? Specifically, will you write and produce the document yourself, or will you hire an outside brochure/public relations consultant to do the job for you? There are advantages to both alternatives.

If you hire an outsider to do the brochure, you will have the time to sell new clients and to service the existing ones. In a busy consulting practice, time has a very definite dollar value, and the cost of doing the brochure yourself is easy to calculate. If you are not busy, your time has a different value; nevertheless, work on the brochure would take you away from efforts to sell new clients.

An outsider will almost certainly complete the brochure before you could yourself. For you, the project will always take second (or even third) place to work you must do for current clients. On the other hand, if you hire someone else to do the project, you can both agree on a deadline, and that will become sacrosanct for your brochure consultant.

Finally, the end project probably will be much better if you have someone else complete the assignment. After all, the reason one hires an outside organization is to benefit from expertise in a particular area.

People who opt to develop their own brochures often choose to do so because it is much less expensive, at least in terms of hard dollars expended, independent of any time value associated with their efforts. Since cash flow is a significant problem in many new consulting situations, anything that minimizes expenditures in the early months is desirable.

Some people develop their own brochures because they have definite ideas and want no independent inputs. For them, involving someone else in the process would be a waste of time and money. Others recognize that they will have to write much of the copy anyway, in order to achieve the copy points and tone they desire, so they feel they might as well do it all themselves.

In reality, however, many consultants combine both approaches, doing pieces of the job themselves and getting professional help for others. Brochure projects subdivide naturally into five phases that can be handled internally or externally, according to individual needs: writing, layout (typestyle, type size, page layout, use of heads and subheads), art direction (the graphic look, color decisions, use of art, placement of noncopy elements, selection of paper/cover stock), mechanical art, and printing and binding.

CONTENT OF A TYPICAL BROCHURE

The following section will review the key parts of any brochure, whether four pages or forty.

Front Cover

The front of the brochure will be seen most; consequently, it should carry out at least three different objectives. It should communicate your practice's company identity to the prospect organization. This is accomplished through the color(s), the graphic design, and the copy. It should also cause the prospect to register the name of your consulting practice in a meaningful way. This is achieved via the size of the name, its position, and the way it is shown on the cover. Some consultants make the mistake of developing a very fancy and eye-catching brochure cover but then putting their name in such small type that it is virtually unreadable and unnoticeable. Finally, the cover should deliver the overall positioning of the organization or, at a minimum, a brief overview of the services you provide. Since the brochure typically will lie flat on a desk, it can be a very effective advertising vehicle, if it is used properly. Therefore, in addition to having a cover that is eye-catching, attractive, and consistent with your overall image, you should add a line or two of copy describing your services. This might be something as simple as your name—say, Weber & Shepherd—followed by an explanatory phrase—perhaps, "Consultants to senior management in executive compensation." Note, in this example, how the company name gains meaning when a descriptive phrase immediately follows it.

Back Cover

There is an almost equal chance that a brochure will end up on a table on its back as on its front. Therefore, the back cover of your brochure also should be able to work effectively for you. You must keep in mind several objectives. First, the back cover should continue the design elements of the front cover. In addition, it should repeat the company name and the brief descriptive line that appears on the front cover. It can also contain some information that might not be appropriate for the front of the brochure, such as your address and phone number, the name of the person to contact for new business inquiries, and a slightly more extensive overview or listing of the major services that your company provides.

Inside Covers

Inside covers can be effective as vehicles to hold other types of material. For example, this could be an excellent way to include personnel bios in a brochure without having to reprint the entire document every time a change occurs. Simply printing the information on a separate page and inserting it in a flap inside the back cover accomplishes a multitude of objectives.

Another type of information that is often incorporated into a brochure in this fashion is the list of clients served. For many consultants, particularly those who are starting out in the business, the list of clients for whom they have worked is their strongest selling point. Normally, these people try to keep their client lists as up-to-date as possible, so they are constantly updating their brochures by inserting new pages that incorporate the very latest additions to their client lists.

Internal Copy

The inside of the brochure should contain at least the following information, organized in a sequence that is logical for your organization.

Company background. The opening paragraphs should provide a very brief overview of your consulting practice, mentioning when it was established and the principal reasons why the business was started.

Mission. The next part of your brochure should contain a broad statement communicating the mission of your organization, written from the perspective of how your business will impact on the client organizations it serves. This should not be the same mission identified in your business plan; rather, it should have direct relevance for a prospect organization that is considering your services.

Services offered. This section should provide a brief overview of the different consulting services that you are prepared to perform for your clients. They should be described concisely and, to the greatest extent possible, in terms of the benefit that the prospect organization will gain from using your organization. In my opinion, one of the biggest mistakes that many organizations make in their communications pieces is to focus on *features* rather than on *benefits*. Prospective buyers are not nearly as interested in what you have to offer as they are in what benefits they will accrue if they retain your service. Consider the example of a person purchasing a drill bit. If one keeps in mind that the person is really purchasing holes and not drills, then the marketing of the drill bit is very different. The buyer simply wants a tool that will give her the best possible hole for the most favorable price and with the least trouble. Any communications to the customer about the drill bit should be made in light of these points. The same principles apply to the consulting business.

Experience. The next part of a brochure should provide some information about the experience or capabilities of you and your organization. You might describe the professional backgrounds of you and your key employees. By demonstrating that you have extensive experience in your area of specialty, you begin to establish the credibility that you need if you are to sell your services. You could also provide examples of projects, industries, or situations in which you and your company have worked that are directly related to your consulting specialty. In this part of the brochure, it is often desirable actually to mention client organizations (if this is common practice in your area of specialty), as well-known company/organization names can add greatly to the overall credibility of your organization.

Success stories. Many consulting companies find it advantageous to include case histories of how clients have benefited from using their services. Normally, these should be very short and should include a brief statement of the situation, consisting of a disguised description of the client organization and the problem that led it to retain your company; a description of what your organization did to solve the problem, including some indication of the time it took; and a summary of the benefits gained by the client organization as a result of your involvement in the project.

In selecting success stories for use in this part of the brochure, it is very important to choose examples to which your prospect universe can relate easily. You should also choose examples that are easy to describe and that you can discuss in more detail with the prospect organization, should they wish to know more about your involvement with the project.

Approach. The next part of the brochure should briefly describe the general way in which you approach consulting assignments. While your actual approaches will differ based on the nature of the projects, this section will communicate nonetheless some broad corporate principles that you have established. This section of the brochure gives you an excellent opportunity to communicate that you, for example, do the following:

- Involve key client personnel throughout the project, in order to arrive at the best possible solution.

- Use a team approach in your organization, in order to insure that the problem at hand benefits from the experience of several different people.

- Place importance on the analytical aspects of the project, in order to develop meaningful conclusions and recommendations. Some people even briefly describe some of the steps that they normally take to uncover the key facts, such as the use of consumer focus groups, quantitative research, field interviews, and so on.

- Keep the client organization involved in the project throughout, in order to ensure that there are no surprises at the conclusion of the assignment. Particularly important to most clients, this is often a vital point to incorporate in this section of the brochure.

Fee structure. It is virtually impossible for most consulting practices to provide a fee schedule in a brochure, as the cost of any assignment depends on a large variety of factors that differ with each project. Still, it is desirable to provide some indication of how your organization establishes fees and what constitutes an average fee (if one can be identified). Some brochures provide a description of a typical assignment and indicate the fees and the time frame associated with it.

Personnel. Somewhere in the brochure (preferably in the back flap as an insert), you should provide background information on the most important people in your organization—names, titles in the company, educational backgrounds, and most relevant work experience (including the names and locations of previous companies, positions in the organization, dates of employment, and key areas of responsibility). Obviously, if you run a one-person organization, you need only to include your own résumé.

Clients served.   A piece that should go in the rear flap of the brochure is a listing of the clients that your company has served in the recent past and is currently serving. This could be a simple listing of the client organizations; a list of the client organizations and the specific divisions (or product areas) where your company has been involved; a list indicating the functional service that you performed for the client (for example, if you performed an executive search for one, compensation consulting for another and outplacement for a third, these would be indicated after the name of the appropriate client organization); or a listing of clients by industry type or by country. Each of these is perfectly acceptable; your choice should depend on personal preference and industry practice in your area of consulting.

The close.   Every brochure should conclude with a section that asks for the order. In essence, this simply indicates that, if the reader is interested in more information about your company, he should contact you (or someone else in the organization) at the specified phone number or address. Most companies also find it helpful to indicate that they will provide a free, no-obligation consultation for the first appointment.

THE BROCHURE DEVELOPMENT PROCESS

The following reviews what I believe is the most effective process for developing a brochure. For the purposes of this discussion, I assume that the document will be developed entirely by you, although most people will job out much of the work.

Step #1.   Conduct a thorough evaluation of other brochures, including those of your competition, people in similar industries, and others in service-oriented businesses. The objective here is to discover what you like and what you do not like about different companies' brochures. You should end up with many items on both sides of the ledger that will be very helpful when you develop your own brochure strategy.

Step #2.   Develop a brochure strategy. As we have mentioned several other times in this book, the first step in any major project should be the development of a strategy. This is the roadmap that assures that you will be where you want to be at the end of the trip. With regard to brochure development, however, this is also the one step that most people fail to execute; they often feel that they already know what they want from their brochures and that developing a strategy would involve superfluous attention to detail and unnecessary sophistication.

I feel strongly that the brochure strategy is the part of the brochure development process that will impact most on the overall quality of the end product. Defining the strategy forces you to think through all important issues ahead of time, allowing you to make decisions based on a careful assessment of the alternatives. The existence of the strategy also virtually guarantees effective communication between you and any other people involved in the development process. Moreover, it should help you to evaluate the various drafts of the brochure, regardless of whether the work has been accomplished internally or by an outside professional organization. The brochure strategy will serve as the standard against which the end product will be measured. Finally, a well-written brochure strategy should also reduce the cost of producing the document. Time and energy will be more targeted, so both internal people and external consultants can work more efficiently.

A well-thought-out brochure strategy should contain the following:

1. A statement of the objectives of the brochure, including target audience definitions, identifying the market segment(s) that the brochure is intended to reach; communications objectives, such as the image, important copy points, and overall message that you wish the brochure to convey; and distribution objectives, intended to identify the basic means by which the brochures will be distributed to the various target audience constituencies

2. Guidelines relative to the cost parameters of developing, printing, and (ultimately) reprinting the brochure

3. Timing considerations, identifying when the document should be completed and how frequently you anticipate changes being

made. This last is very important as it will affect the choice of binding and often determine whether a flap will be added to the back of the brochure to hold frequently updated information

4. A discussion of special needs, such as the need for special colors, the desire to have special die cuts in the cover or the inside portions of the brochure, or the need for pockets to carry material that changes frequently

5. Executional considerations, such as the use of color(s) versus black and white, the use of photos, line art, graphs, tables, or other similar noncopy elements, and the trim size of the brochure

6. Creative considerations, such as the tone of the copy, a specific listing of the most important copy points that must be developed in the brochure, and guidance regarding the extent to which the brochure should be descriptive (i.e., wordy) or brief

Step #3. Work up a rough outline. Summarize the most important general topic areas that you want to cover in the brochure.

Step #4. Check the overall flow and the content. Arrange the various topics in the outline in a sequence that seems logical for the final document. Then read through all the headline ideas that have been identified for the various sections, to confirm that the document covers all important points in an order that makes sense.

Step #5. Write body copy. Once you are comfortable with the flow of the major ideas and are sure that all the issues are covered, it is time to begin to develop the copy points for each of the major headlines. This is a very difficult part of the process as there is a natural tendency to write much more than is absolutely needed. The objective should be to use the fewest possible words to communicate effectively the copy points outlined in the brochure strategy.

Step #6. Get input from others regarding the copy content. After you are happy with the content of the brochure, it is a very good idea to give the document to a few people whose opinions you respect, in order to get their impressions. If these people take sufficient time with the brochure, you can get some very valuable input.

Step #7. Revise the brochure copy based on the comments obtained. After you have received all inputs, you should modify the copy to reflect the best suggestions.

Step #8. Develop a graphic look for the brochure. Once the copy content is finalized, you should begin to finalize the look of the brochure. For this part of the process, most people work with an outside consultant/graphic designer, who normally will have a much better feeling than you for the most effective ways to use art and graphics.

Step #9. Obtain a dummy comp of the brochure for others to review before you proceed to a final mechanical. In essence, the objective here is to get a semi-finished document that you can expose to others whom you respect for their business and communications opinions, in order to check out both the copy and the graphics before you actually go to press.

Step #10. Move to mechanical art. The last stage of the graphics process is the development of the mechanical by a mechanical artist who knows how best to render the document that you have provided in a comp/dummy form. It is very expensive to change anything in the mechanical stage, so it is very important that you be very comfortable with the brochure before you begin this phase of the process.

Step #11. Get the document printed. After the mechanical has been completed and approved, the brochure is ready to be printed. Mechanical artists often can help with this part of the effort, as they normally will know most of the printers in the area that can handle the job. It is always a good idea to ask several (two to four) different printers for estimates, since costs often vary considerably from company to company. When you evaluate the bids, however, be sure to compare all the same specifications, relating to such things as the cover stock, the interior stock, quantities, timing, and so on.

DISTRIBUTION

On completion of the production process, you may wonder what you should do with the hundreds (or thousands) of brochures that you now have on hand. First, you should mail copies to all your current and former clients, who generally will be very interested in your brochure. With each brochure, include a letter indicating that you hope that your new brochure will give the recipient a better understanding of the full range of services that your company provides. The main purpose for sending brochures to these people is to help maintain a high level of awareness for your company; with luck, it will also stimulate some additional work as clients learn about the broad range of your services. You should also try to get copies of the brochure into the hands of any other people who are still high-potential prospects for consulting assignments. Again, the purpose is to increase the awareness of your organization but also to communicate the variety of services you offer so that prospects will consider you for other types of work, in the event the current project is awarded to someone else.

In both instances, it is a very good idea to ask recipients for their opinions of the piece. If you are aware of the strengths and weaknesses of the existing brochure, you will be able to improve it in future printings.

SUMMARY

The brochure is probably the most controversial part of the entire marketing plan for a consulting practice, because it is viewed by many as being so important and, therefore, given high priority during the start-up phase of a practice. In reality, the brochure is relatively unimportant for most consulting practices, and it should not consume your time and energy. This is not to suggest that you should not have a brochure but, rather, that you should think through your needs very carefully before you get started. The brochure is probably most valuable in the consulting sales process, and you should determine how you will handle this process before you make any final decisions about the brochure.

10 Selling Your Consulting Services

The bottom line in the consulting business is knowing how to sell business. Many consultants feel that being a salesperson is beneath them and that they should not have to sell to generate business. Unfortunately, this is almost never the case. You can be the best consultant in the world, but, if you are unable to sell business, you will not make a living: Consulting must be sold like any other product or service.

There is a well-known saying that salesmen are born, not made. On the whole, I agree—sales skills differ significantly among people; some have an innate knack and feel for sales; others simply have little talent in this area. This chapter provides some general guidelines about the consulting sales process that will be helpful to all salespeople, whether natural or developed. The process is relatively simple and, if followed, will generate sales for your practice. Clearly, some people will be more effective than others, but you can be sure that if you follow the principles of selling outlined in this chapter, your success ratio will improve significantly.

ELEMENTS OF THE SALES PROCESS

There are five key steps in the selling process (see Figure 10.1). The remainder of this chapter will discuss in detail what you can do to

143

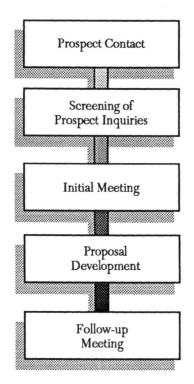

Figure 10.1. The Five-Step Process for Selling Consulting Services

maximize the effectiveness of your approach during the first three of these phases. Chapter 11 will cover the remaining two.

Prospect Contact

The first part of the selling process consists of your initial contact with the prospect. The way this contact is initiated and the events during the first three to five minutes of the relationship influence very significantly the likelihood of your obtaining the consulting assignment.

In my experience, the probability of entering into a consulting relationship with a prospect is dramatically greater when the potential client initiates the first contact. I would estimate that the chances of signing a consulting contract might be ten to twenty times greater if this is the case. First of all, when the prospect organization contacts you, it has an idea that it might wish to hire a consultant. Often, it is only an idea, and the phone call (or letter) is just a fishing trip to compare the costs or capabilities of various organizations or even to fulfill multiple bidding requirements. Still, the fact that the prospect has identified the possibility of a need for your services represents a giant step in the right direction. Moreover, when the prospect organization contacts you, it normally has some information about your company, and you begin the conversation with some credibility. This also is an advantage you would not have enjoyed had you initiated the contact. Finally, when the prospect organization contacts you, it often specifies when it needs to get a proposal and when it needs to have the prospective assignment completed. This also is a major benefit to you, as it establishes a time frame for the relationship. If you make the initial contact, the prospect organization does not normally have any time sequence in mind, since it probably was not thinking about hiring a consultant before you got in touch.

Despite the very meaningful advantages associated with prospect organizations making the initial contact, some disadvantages do go along with this alternative. First, you do not have any control over whether the people who contact you are viable consulting clients. It is possible to waste a significant amount of time with people on the telephone and even with follow-up letters or meetings, only to find that they are not viable clients because of their size, their demands, or the personalities in the organization.

Second, you do not have any control over when people contact you, and therefore it is often necessary to drop everything in the midst of a current client rush, just to spend time on the telephone with a prospective client who has contacted you. This can significantly affect your ability to complete work for existing clients, which must take priority.

Finally, one of the biggest disadvantages is that it is not unusual for prospect organizations to call consultants under the guise of needing help but really only wanting to discuss their ideas and get your preliminary reactions, generally at no cost. Anybody who has been in the consulting business for a reasonable period of time can count numerous occasions when they have been ripped off by a prospect organization that asked for a proposal without ever intending to hire a consultant.

What, then, can you do to protect your time when you receive inquiries for potential consulting assignments? Basically, there are two key factors to consider, both of which will be covered in the discussion of the second (screening) stage of the sales process.

Once contact has been made, the first few minutes of the interaction may determine whether the contact translates into a consulting contract.

First, show enthusiasm about having received the call. Even before you ascertain whether a contact will be of interest to you, it is important to act as though you are very glad that the prospect has called to seek your involvement.

Second, unless it is absolutely impossible, take the call immediately and handle what needs to be accomplished during this initial contact. Some people can focus on only one thing at a time and have great difficulty stopping what they are doing in order to deal with a new business inquiry. However, from the psychological perspective of prospects contacting you, it is much better to take a few minutes to talk with them while the issue is on their minds, rather than putting them off until it is more convenient for you. By talking to them immediately, you communicate to them that they are important to you, even if you do not know what their needs are at the present time. You also use your time more efficiently, as you will not need to track them down later. In the current environment, where meetings take up so much of everyone's time, it is better to try to finish your business with someone while you have them on the telephone instead of playing telephone tag trying to get back to them.

Third, prepare a very concise way of describing the nature of your consulting business and the scope of your operations. Normally, this will be the first thing that a prospect wants to know. A well-rehearsed and carefully thought-through explanation of the services you provide will make a very professional first impression.

Fourth, remain constantly aware that the impressions you make during the first few minutes of a conversation can be vital and will often decide whether further discussion will occur. Be sure to use a friendly voice on the telephone and communicate an attitude that indicates you are concerned about the needs of the caller, even if your organization will not be able to help. You never know who prospects know or who might ask them about your company in the future, so try to build goodwill for your consulting organization with all callers, regardless of their potential as clients.

Finally, try your hardest to help callers complete their missions (i.e., find a consultant), even if you are not the right person for them. To this end, it is generally a good idea to refer calls to other consultants or to a resource that will help them find a consultant in the event you cannot be of help.

Screening of Prospect Inquiries

As indicated previously, a key to the selling process is insuring that the inquiries you allocate time to are valid prospects and that others are disposed of in an appropriate manner. The trick here is to identify true potential clients, without turning off others whom you feel are not valid but might turn out to be. Therefore, when you receive a call, your objective is to determine quickly whether the caller is a legitimate prospect, and, if so, to gather some basic information that will enable you to prepare for the upcoming meeting with the individual to discuss your potential involvement.

Step #1. Determine the prospect's validity as a prospective client. Early in the initial telephone call, you should try to find out where the caller got your name. This is often the most revealing tip-off as to the viability of the inquiry, as some referral sources are much more productive than others. For example, the Yellow Pages are probably the lowest level of referral that you can handle. As discussed earlier in the chapters on awareness building, the Yellow Pages are normally a viable source of leads for only a few types of consulting practices. If a caller got your name from the Yellow Pages, it is unlikely that he or she will know much about your capabilities and probably will be very unsophisticated regarding the use of consultants.

If the caller indicates that he or she got your name from a trade association or a trade association directory, he or she may be a viable prospect, but these sources suggest that the caller probably is shopping around for consultants. Also, they normally indicate that a caller is not particularly versed in the use of consultants, which could require you to do a good deal of educating before you are successful in signing a contract.

If the individual called as a result of reading an article (or book) you have written or hearing a speech you have given, this can often be a very strong lead. The prospect is coming into the conversation with the feeling that you offer something that will fill a specific need, which certainly makes for a good beginning.

If the referral comes from a former (or current) client, it normally is the best of all situations. First, it suggests that the caller has done some research before calling you and probably knows a good deal about you and your capabilities. Second, the chances are that the caller talked with the referrer about you and thus enters the conversation with a predisposition to employ your services. This type of inquiry deserves immediate and concentrated action.

Another thing you should pay attention to during the initial contact is the caller's approach to the inquiry. For example, if a prospect organization identifies a specific problem that it wants to fix, this represents a very positive situation, since it indicates that the prospect organization has taken the time to think through its needs. If the problem is well defined, this tells you that the prospect organization probably understands how to use consultants effectively or at least knows something about the process.

If, on the other hand, the reason for the call is poorly defined, it is significantly less likely that the contact will result in a consulting contract. You will have to work with the prospect to define the problem; this takes time and, unless it is handled very well by you, can be a difficult process that might conclude with the prospect organization deciding not to hire a consultant at all.

Finally, you should determine whether the caller has prior experience using a consultant. In my experience, the best prospects are those that have used consultants in the past. They understand what is involved in using a consultant and how a consultant can contribute most effectively to the organization. They also are aware of the costs associated with using a consultant. Cost is a big concern for first-time users; with repeat users, cost is usually much less of an issue.

Step #2. Gather sufficient information about the prospective assignment and the client organization for you to conduct an effective introductory meeting. Once you have determined that the caller represents a viable prospect that should be pursued further, your objective should be to collect the information that will help you in the subsequent steps of the sales process. This should include

1. Some very brief background about the company and the situation that led to the consideration of outside consulting services. This will be helpful to you during the preplanning phase of the third part of the sales process, the initial meeting. Specifically, you should ask about the nature of the business, the product or

service involved, and any past attempts to solve the problem for which your help has been sought.

2. The expectations of the caller relative to this meeting. Specifically, what would the prospect like to accomplish when you follow up the call with a visit. This information will influence greatly how you plan the presentation.

3. The timing for the initial meeting, the follow-up proposal, and the completion of the assignment, should you become involved.

4. Who will be attending the meeting, and whether they are decision-makers in their organization. The latter part of this question needs to be handled very carefully, since some callers may perceive it as lessening their role in selecting the consultant.

5. How long the meeting—including both the formal presentation and the follow-up questions—should last.

6. Where and when will the meeting be held. The time and place of a meeting is very important to the overall effectiveness of a presentation. Generally, you should avoid meetings very late in the afternoon (particularly on Friday) or right after lunch. Also, some consultants are better off holding meetings in their own offices, as they can bring in several other people and perhaps show off an attractive facility, whereas other consultants are best served by going to the client's premises.

A final consideration in this area is to ensure that the meeting room is large enough and equipped properly (i.e., with overhead projectors, VCRs, etc.) for your presentation.

Once all this information is collected, you are ready for the third step in the selling process.

The Initial Meeting

The third major part of the selling process is the initial meeting, which normally will be your first face-to-face contact with the prospect organization. Your primary objective during the initial meeting is to sell yourself and your company to the prospect organization so that it will want to hire you as a consultant. By the end of the meeting, the only details that should need to be determined are the scope of the project, the costs of your services, and the schedule. (You will find that, if you have effectively sold yourself, the prospect organization will be much less likely to quibble about the costs of hiring you.)

During this meeting, you should also learn enough about the client situation to be in a position to determine the following information

- How to approach the project for maximum effectiveness on your part and the best results for the prospect organization.

- Whether, based on the technical skills needed, the scope of what is required, the funds available for consulting services, and the timing required for the final report, you want to do the assignment.

- How much time will be required for you to complete the assignment.

The part of the sales process concerned with the initial meeting actually involves six separate phases—preparation, introductions, the presentation, information gathering, the close, and finally, the exit (see Figure 10.2).

Preparation. The preparation phase is absolutely essential to get you ready for the coming meeting. As in any sale, the more information you have about the situation you are entering, the more successful will be your sales call. During the preparation phase, you will arm yourself with the information that will maximize your effectiveness in the meeting. You will also check that the logistics of the meeting are complete and appropriate to your planned presentation. Last, you will orchestrate the actual meeting, from the position of the salesperson, to increase the overall effectiveness of the presentation.

To achieve these objectives, the preparation phase should contain the following three basic elements:

1. *Research.* Prior to the meeting, you will want to do some basic research so that you will be able to ask relevant (and well-thought-out) questions during the meeting and demonstrate to the prospect organization that you have done some homework. This research will differ depending on the type of meeting that

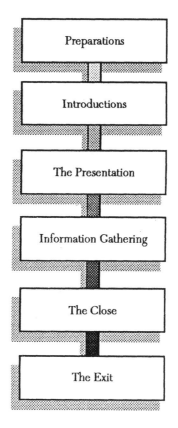

Figure 10.2. The Six Stages of the Initial Meeting

is planned and your overall familiarity with the prospect company and its industry; in most cases, however, you will look for basic background about the company, the division, and the product/service line that will be the focus for the meeting and for information about the people with whom you will be working should the meeting prove productive. This is why it is so important for you to ask the right questions in the screening phase, in order to narrow down the topic so that research can be highly focused. The key is to establish whether there are any particular issues relating to the industry, the company, and the product line that are germane to the discussion that will occur at the meeting. Further, it is always beneficial to know your target audience, and the more you know about them, the better prepared you will be to sell effectively. The best way to obtain this type of information is to talk with people who have had business dealings with the individuals with whom you will be meeting, such as former employees of the company, their suppliers, or even noncompetitive consultants who have done or tried to do business with them.

Your research should also provide you with some indication as to the key leverage points in the business that drive volume and profitability. For example, it would be very helpful to enter a meeting knowing that the most important element of the prospect's marketing mix is pricing or that the business is sales driven. An understanding of these types of factors will impact on your ability to be effective in the meeting.

Another objective of the research phase is to identify a few key areas of questioning, so that you can demonstrate an active interest in the assignment. There are many different ways to obtain this information; the most common sources are industry publications and relevant trade associations. Often, a database search of the company and its industry will provide you with what you need.

2. *Logistics.* One of the keys to your logistics review is to make sure that you have enough time to prepare for the meeting and that you fully understand what the client expects from you. One of the most valuable lessons I learned early in my consulting career is "Never present until you are ready." While you certainly want to accommodate the needs of the prospect, it is usually better to postpone your presentation until you can be effective than to perform in less than a satisfactory mode. (Sometimes, of course, it will not be possible to postpone a meeting, and, in those cases, you should try to do the best you can.) The objective is always to give yourself as much of an advantage as possible, in terms of both your own level of preparedness and the general logistics of the meeting, such as location, time available, people present, and the like. An effective seller of consulting services will check and recheck the logistics of a meeting to ensure the best possible selling environment.

3. *Presentation mechanics.* The final part of the preparation phase involves decisions regarding the actual presentation and might include such things as the following:

- Deciding who from your organization should attend the meeting. If you operate a one-person consulting company, you should decide whether you should bring another person with you—perhaps a subcontractor or an associate with whom you will work on the assignment. My experience strongly favors two people in a new business presentation, as one can be presenting/talking while the other is thinking or preparing to answer questions. Further, with another person in attendance, you will give the prospect organization the impression that you represent more than a solo consulting company, which normally will be more to your advantage.

- Determining who will give various parts of the presentation. My experience is that the best presenters should do the presenting, almost regardless of where they fit into the consulting organization hierarchy. Many successful consultants are not good presenters, so they leave the selling to others who are better in this area. Often, a very senior person will open a meeting with a few introductory remarks, then let a more junior associate make the actual presentation.

- Deciding how much of the actual presentation should be boilerplate, and how much needs to be tailored to the specific needs of the prospect organization. Obviously, it is always better to tailor as much as possible to the organization with whom you are meeting; however, this is not always possible due to time constraints or informational inadequacies.

Introductions. The introductions that occur at the start of the meeting represent a very small part of the entire selling process; nevertheless, they are crucial, since they can set the tone for everything that follows. You must be sure to meet and make eye contact with each person in attendance and to understand the position held by each of the attendees, so that you will know who are the decision makers and who are the key influencers. You also need to ensure that everyone in attendance knows who you are, who your associates are, and what role you play in the consulting organization.

Try not to begin the meeting until everyone is present: It is extremely distracting to begin a meeting only to be interrupted by late arrivals. Then, as soon as you can, exchange business cards with everyone in attendance. This way, they will know who you are and the others in your group are and what role each of you plays in your organization. You will also have the correct names and titles of all the people in the room before the session begins. (I have found that placing the business cards on the table in a pattern that echoes the seating helps me attach the names with the faces during the course of the meeting.)

With regard to exchanging business cards, there actually is a right and a wrong way to go about it. Taking someone's card and immediately putting it in your pocket or briefcase can send a message that the person is not very important to you. On the other hand, if you take the business card in your hand and spend a few seconds looking at it (some even believe you should caress it a little), you send a nonverbal message of caring.

Once these preliminaries are over, begin the meeting by introducing yourself and any others in your party and encouraging the prospect organization to do the same thing. With these careful introductions, you will be able to tailor some of your comments to particular people, based on their functions in the organization or their roles in the decision-making process.

The presentation.   There are some general questions that you need to answer before you can actually write an effective sales presentation. For example, what type of information should you include in the presentation to make your selling effort most effective? How long should the formal presentation last, and how much time should you leave for other aspects of the meeting? What medium should you use to present to the prospect organization? Should you plan a very formal meeting with 35-mm slides, an informal meeting with overhead projector acetates, or something in between? All of these questions need to be addressed before you can begin to develop the presentation. The answers will differ according to the client situation, the principal variables being such things as

- The size of the meeting. If it is a large group, you will need projection equipment so that everyone can see the material that you present.

- The current knowledge of your company among the people in attendance. If they are familiar with you, then you need not devote much time to presenting your credentials; however, if you are new to them, you will need to build your credibility with a very persuasive overview of your company and its capabilities.

- The levels of the people that will be in attendance. If very senior people will be at the meeting, you might want to make the presentation more formal (but probably less detail oriented) than you would if more junior people were present.

- The amount of time you have to complete the task at hand. Often, this factor most dictates the scope and content of the presentation.

- The place where the meeting will be held and what presentation facilities will be available. For example, if the meeting is held over a dinner table, the nature of the presentation will be very different than it would be in a conference room.

Even with all if the variables that affect the content of a stand-up presentation, some basic information should be included in most new business presentations.

1. *Credentials presentation.* During the first part of the presentation, you should build credibility for your organization by providing the prospect with a significant amount of information about you and your company.

   - *Company background.* Give some background on your company. Outline when it was founded, what its current structure is, and where the office(s) are located.

   - *Category and client history.* Next, you should cover the product/service categories in which your company has experience, to establish your company's track record and display the breadth and depth of its experience. If you are just starting out as a consultant, you could summarize your most relevant experience as a "client," focusing on those aspects of your background that most overlap the interests of the prospect organization.

- *Personnel.* You should also provide a brief biographical sketch of the people in your organization—their educational backgrounds, prior work histories (i.e., companies, positions, and dates), other relevant accomplishments (i.e., key publications, positions held in major industry associations, etc.), and current positions in your organization.

2. *Scope of the practice.* Next, you should give the prospect organization an overview of the functional areas in which your consulting organization practices. Cover every major area of your involvement, even if all of them are not directly related to the needs of the prospect company: By describing all the things your company does, you may evoke some interest in using your practice in other projects.

3. *Relevance.* At this point, you should outline the scope of selected projects that you have accomplished that are directly relevant to the assignment in question. Mention other work you have done in the prospect organization's industry and in very related industries. You should also describe work you have done in functional areas that relate closely to the work that would be involved in the potential assignment. For example, if the proposed project is the development of a compensation system for long-haul truck drivers and you have never done this type of project in the past, you might cite compensation programs you have developed for other similar industry groups, in order to demonstrate your capabilities in this area.

4. *Case history.* Some consulting organizations find that one of the most effective ways to present their credentials is to provide brief case histories of past consulting assignments. Typically, these are blind (i.e., the client is unidentified), and they are set up in the following format:

- Statement of the problem
- Outline of the solution that was proposed
- Summary of the results

5. *Typical project implementation procedures.* Now, you should provide a brief description of the normal process that your consulting organization follows to implement an assignment. While the steps in the process can vary somewhat depending on the assignment, most consultants apply some basic guidelines consistently across projects.

6. *Staffing and costing.* Finally, you should furnish an overview of your approach to staffing a consulting assignment. For example, which of the representatives attending the meeting from your organization would be directly involved in the consulting assignment, and what would be each person's role in the project? If others are likely to be involved, how would they fit into the project team? (These others might be people from outside your company—other consulting associates, suppliers, etc.—who form part of your project implementation team.) At this time, you should also discuss your approach to costing consulting projects. Explain briefly how you arrive at your consulting fees and what other costs are incremental to that fee (i.e., travel, entertainment, messenger service, long distance telephone, etc.).

At the conclusion of the stand-up presentation, you must ask the people in attendance if they learned enough about your company. It is vital to get any outstanding questions on the table at this time, or they will linger in peoples' minds and may create problems for you in the future. The following are typical of the questions that come up at this stage:

- How does your company handle competitive conflicts?
- What is your policy regarding confidentiality of information gained as a result of a consulting assignment?
- How long do you usually take to complete a consulting assignment?
- What would you say is the cost of a typical consulting project?
- Why is your company the best choice for this assignment?
- What are your concerns about being able to handle this assignment so that it will achieve our objectives?
- Will you work with us under a contingency arrangement by

which you will get paid only if some specific predetermined result is achieved?

All of the above, plus many others that you probably conjure, may require your attention at an initial presentation meeting. It is always better to anticipate questions in advance of the meeting, so that you will be able to handle them effectively if they are asked. Consequently, for the most generic questions, it is strongly suggested that you actually write down answers before the meeting, as this exercise will help you to think through the best possible answers.

Information gathering. During the presentation, you should try to gather as much information as possible so that you will be able to develop an effective proposal. This process will also build your credibility if you ask intelligent, well-thought-out questions that demonstrate that you have done your homework relative to the prospective assignment.

There are several things that you must do in the course of the meeting if you are to gather enough information to write a proposal.

1. Ensure that the prospect organization provides you with sufficient background information about their business and the problem(s) for which they are seeking outside assistance. In many areas of the consulting industry, it is possible to develop a proposal based on the input from the initial meeting and some additional follow-up research in secondary source literature. However, sometimes, you need to meet with other people in the client organization before you can write a proposal. If so, it is essential to discuss this in the meeting and to make arrangements to take that second step, so that you can move to the proposal stage as soon as possible.

2. Obtain an agreement as to the scope of the assignment. This is a vital part of the meeting, as it will enable you to focus your proposal on the areas of the prospect organization's operation that require the most help. However, for this agreement, it is necessary to have an open discussion to identify what the client organization's expectations are regarding your involvement. This subject is best handled in the initial presentation meeting, in order to minimize the chances of some of the client people coming back to you after the proposal is written to indicate that it is not what they had expected.

3. Determine the prospect organization's timing needs. This relates both to when it wishes to receive the proposal and when it requires the actual project to be completed. Timing will have a significant impact on the content (and probably the cost) of your proposal.

4. Try to obtain a budget or, at least an estimate of what the client organization has set aside for the project. The more accurate this information is, the more targeted your proposal can be.

5. Identify what the prospect organization is seeking in terms of a format for the proposal. Some companies require very detailed proposals that outline all the steps of the project and any aspect that will impact on the costs, whereas others only want a one-page written summary of the objectives of the assignment, what you will accomplish, and what your involvement will cost.

The close. After the information-gathering section of the meeting is over, you will move into the close. Like the introductions, this normally takes only a few minutes but is a vital part of the entire process. During this portion of the meeting, you should make sure that the people in attendance have learned as much as they wish about you and your organization. It is essential that you ask the assembled group this question directly, to ensure that all needs are met in this area. At the same time, you should verify that you have enough information to develop an effective proposal. This is difficult as you must think about all the information that you have accumulated, identify the areas that you will need to cover in the proposal, and then review all this data for any gaps that need to be filled before you leave the meeting. You also need to secure agreement from the people in the prospect organization as to the next steps that will occur and what their timing will be. You should find out whom in the client organization you could contact over the next few days should you need additional information in order to prepare your proposal. Finally, you should ask the client organization about the decision process and time frame for the assignment. The client should be willing to tell you what process it will use to select a consulting organization and when it anticipates a decision.

The exit. The final part of the initial presentation is the exit. Many salespeople overlook this part of the selling process, but I have found that it can be extremely important. Essentially, it consists of three basic elements:

1. *The final words.* Take a sentence or two to express to the people in attendance your pleasure at having the opportunity of presenting to them and your enthusiasm about the possibility of working with them. The intent is to end the meeting on a very positive note and to leave the people with favorable feelings about you and your company.

2. *Materials distribution.* Make sure that everyone in attendance receives any presentation materials that you have prepared. Handing them out personally gives you a chance to make one final eye contact with each person and thank each one very quickly for participating in the meeting.

3. *Departure.* Some consulting assignments are lost, even before the proposal has been written, because of sloppy departures. The key is to go quickly; do not linger around the client's premises making small talk or having private meetings. Most clients appreciate it when a consulting organization is respectful of their time and leaves promptly when the meeting is completed. This is a small thing, but it can be a very meaningful irritant if you do not handle it properly.

SUMMARY

The consulting sales process involves five very distinct phases, all of which must be followed for the effort to have the maximum impact. The objective of this chapter was to familiarize you with the first three of these steps, in preparation for the important information that will be covered in the next chapter: the development of the consulting proposal and the execution of the follow-up. It is essential for you to understand that, unless you do a good job with the sales process, you will never get to the stage of proposal development.

11 The Consulting Proposal

The development of the proposal is the end point of the new business process, and it will ultimately determine whether you are successful in selling the project. Before you begin to develop the proposal, you should go through a preparatory stage to verify that the proposal is on target relative to the needs of the prospect organization. Most of the elements of this stage can be covered at the close of the initial meeting or handled a few days later in a one-to-one conversation with a client contact. When it should occur will depend on the receptiveness of the group assembled at the initial meeting toward this type of detailed discussion. My experience indicates that it normally is best for you and the person to whom the proposal will be written to take care of this step after the meeting (either immediately or a day or two later).

During this stage, it is essential to find out exactly when the client organization needs the proposal. This allows you to budget your time effectively. For example, if you have (what you feel is) a lot of time, it is often a good idea to tell the prospect contact that you would like to write the proposal and send it to him first so that you can obtain his views/comments on the content and methodology. This generally will result in a proposal that is more tailored to the prospect organization's needs, which, ideally, will increase your chances of getting the assignment. It also averts the danger that your proposal will contain any errors of fact that would reduce your credibility in the eyes of the prospect organization. Often, these errors can occur in the background section of a proposal, when you are recalling the circumstances that led the prospect organization to consider an outside consulting organization.

By involving the prospect contact in the proposal before you release it to the organization, you obtain a psychological buy-in from this person regarding the work you are proposing. He will feel that he has participated in the proposal development and has a stake in what you are saying. The extent to which you can get this emotional commitment from the prospect contact can have a dramatic effect on the success of your proposal.

In the event that you do not have time to go through this process, at least you will know what your deadline is so that you can submit the proposal on time. My experience suggests that you should always try to deliver the proposal one or two days ahead of the due date, but *not* before that. If you submit the proposal ahead of time, the client organization can get the impression that you have not spent enough time thinking about it. Clearly, this is an impression you want to avoid.

A major mistake that you can make is to write a proposal in a format that does not meet the prospect organization's specific needs. Some companies prefer very brief, written proposals, almost outlines; others are satisfied with a verbal proposal, followed by a confirming letter if your proposition is accepted; still others are interested in a detailed proposal.

In most consulting situations, I strongly favor the use of the detailed proposal; however, both the verbal approach and the short letter also have their advantages. For example, with the more abbreviated approaches, the prospect organization finds out the price and scope of the consulting job much more quickly than it would otherwise, without having to wade through reams of paperwork. The consultant, on the other hand, invests far less time and money with these options, as there is no (or little) writing, typing, or mailing/faxing time involved. The third potential advantage of this approach is that some consultants are much more convincing verbally than they are in writing and therefore might offer a better proposal to the prospect organization.

The detailed written proposal represents the other end of the spectrum. Certainly, such a proposal is much more time-consuming to review, but it also gives the prospect organization an opportunity to see how well the consultant can communicate his or her ideas in writing. Since so much of the work of consulting is presented on paper, this is a skill that prospect organizations value. The detailed proposal also enables the prospect organization to have a complete understanding of the work you are proposing; it should leave no questions as to your estimation of the scope and timing of the overall assignment and the individual steps in each stage of the process.

Because of this, it will be much easier for your prospect contact to communicate the content of your proposal to others in the organization who need to be involved in the decision-making process.

Some consultants will not submit a detailed proposal without being paid for the time, while many prospect organizations will not want to incur costs for the assignment before the project has even begun. This can constitute a considerable disadvantage for both: The consultant may lose the opportunity to bid on a project; the prospect may exclude excellent candidates.

The detailed proposal does provide you with a chance to sell your capabilities directly to each of the people who will be exposed to the proposal. It does not leave the selling up to the prospect contact, nor does it limit the basis for consultant selection to price. Indeed, an effective proposal can be the difference between a successful and unsuccessful sales effort.

The detailed proposal also serves as somewhat of an insurance policy, as it outlines the specific scope of the assignment. If you get the job and the client then indicates that it wants you to do a, b, and c, the proposal will spell out the agreed-upon score of the project. These same specifics will provide you with a work plan in the event the proposal is accepted. Often, considerable time passes between the submission of a proposal and the start of a project, and, generally, you will be involved with many other assignments during that period. If a detailed proposal exists, you can simply read the original document when it is time to begin work on the new project, instead of attempting to reconstruct it from memory.

A detailed proposal also allows you to develop realistic costs for the project. This is not to suggest that you need to develop a detailed proposal to cost out an assignment accurately; however, my experience suggests that the probability of this happening is much greater if the proposal is written with some detail as to the project's scope and approach.

The formal written proposal does carry some disadvantages for the consultant. Some people in the client organization will not read a long document, so writing a detailed proposal can be a waste of time and energy. This is a particular concern in the case of very senior people, who often refuse to read long proposal documents. Long proposals also take time to develop, which is expensive. Finally, they can pose problems for busy consultants, since the writing process takes them away from active client projects, the revenue-generating portions of the business.

Before you begin the proposal, you must also decide the form in which it will appear. For example, should it be in the form of a letter or in a presentation format? The letter format is self-explanatory and can often be used very effectively for simple proposals. The presentation format, in which the various parts of the proposal usually are covered in separate, self-contained sections then bound together, is a more formal approach to proposal development and is generally preferable for longer, more complex presentations. You also must ask yourself whether the presentation should be simple or fancy. Some consultants go to great expense to provide prospect organizations with proposals with fancy tabs, color headings, and other such embellishments, bound in very elaborate binders. This approach appeals to some organizations, but for others, it is a very serious mistake, as some people may feel that the fancy package exists to cover up a lack of substance. It is important to try to figure out how the prospect organization feels about the use of fancy proposals before you submit one. Further, you should think very carefully how that type of presentation fits with your corporate identity before you consider it as an alternative.

STRUCTURE OF AN EFFECTIVE CONSULTING PROPOSAL

This section of the chapter provides a construct for a proposal outline that will apply to most types of consulting, yet is sufficiently broad that additional sections can easily be added to adapt the general outline to almost any consulting practice. The proposal outline I feel is best consists of ten different sections. These are discussed below.

Section 1. The Opening

The consulting proposal should start with a sentence that indicates to the reader the precise reason for the communication. A typical lead-in might be "The purpose of this letter is to provide the RMG company with a formal proposal outlining how GLD Inc. will be of assistance in the area of developing a marketing plan for the introduction of new Scrongy Soap." This opening normally would go on to indicate how the proposal came about and might read something like "This follows up the meeting we held at your offices on January 3, in which you outlined the nature of the new product introduction and the areas in which you feel outside consulting assistance might be needed."

Section 2. Background

This next section outlines the key factual information that was provided to you in the briefing for the potential consulting assignment. It should include background about the project for which you are developing the proposal and the thinking of the management group at the prospect organization regarding the need for outside consulting services. The objectives of this section are:

- To communicate to the prospect organization that you are sufficiently familiar with the facts associated with the project to develop a consulting proposal

- To show that the proposal is based on the correct assumptions about the prospect organization's requirements for the consulting engagement

- To ensure that all parties in the prospect organization who read the proposal have sufficient background about what has been said to you and what has been requested of you to be able to evaluate your submission fairly

One of the biggest issues that you must resolve is how long and detailed this section should be. There are several schools of thought about this, with some people thinking it should be very brief and others feeling that it should be very detailed.

Those people who recommend the brief approach prefer it because they feel that a shorter document is more likely to be read completely by all of the appropriate people. Also, they think that it is sufficient to give the prospect organization an overview of what they have said, since they already know the material and the objective is only to communicate to them that they were understood.

The proponents of detailed backgrounds, on the other hand, feel that, because this approach communicates to the client in detail all the facts that one has assimilated in the course of developing the proposal, it proves that no misinterpretations of the facts have occurred. The detail background section also demonstrates to the prospect organization the consultant's ability to grasp a lot of material very quickly and to present it in an organized fashion.

Section 3. Objective(s) of the Assignment

This very succinct and precise statement should indicate to the prospect organization in a very simple fashion what you plan to have achieved by the end of the consulting engagement. The objectives should be stated from the most general to the most specific in a logical order that reflects your priorities.

It is very important for the objectives included in the proposal to be realistic, accurate, and measurable. For example, if the objective of the Scrongy Soap introduction is to generate a 3 percent market share and the marketing plan is aimed at that goal, it would be a mistake to state that the objective of the consulting assignment is to develop a marketing plan that will generate a 3 percent share of the children's soap category. If the actual share level is not an appropriate objective, one might express the objective as being

- to generate a marketing plan for Scrongy Soap that is based on the brand achieving a 3 percent share of the market at the end of year one;

- to develop marketing programs for the introduction of Scrongy Soap within a budget of x dollars; or

- to provide specific implementation details as part of the plan, so that the client organization can immediately begin implementing the plan once it has been approved.

The key to the objectives section is clarity, so that everyone reading the document will know exactly what the proposal is all about.

Section 4. Scope of the Engagement

This part of the proposal is intended to communicate to the prospect organization what the consulting assignment will cover, so there are no questions later on as to what the assignment entails. For example, in the case of the Scrongy Soap plan, this section might specify which aspects of the marketing mix would be included and which would not. Perhaps the client organization does not need the consulting group to work on the advertising copy or media development because it already has an effective advertising agency, or maybe it does not want the consulting group involved in pricing. On the other hand, it might want considerable help in determining the most effective sales and distribution organization to handle the product and in identifying the compensation and incentive programs that would motivate this group.

The scope section must outline in as much detail as possible all the areas that the consultant will become involved in during the course of an assignment. In the case of a very broad consulting assignment (such as an analysis of the poor performance of a division of the client company), this section can be vital for communicating to the organization what you will and will not be doing and gives you a chance to modify the project scope to match the desires/anticipations of the prospect organization.

Section 5. Approach to the Assignment

This section explains to the prospect organization how the assignment will be worked. Outline in chronological order each major task that you will perform in order to deliver the assignment that has been promised in the objectives section of the document. You should also provide the prospect organization with an overview of the steps that you will take to gather the information you need to conduct the assignment and evaluate the inputs for presentation to the client. Some examples of the types of inputs that are often described in this section are listed here:

- Primary research that will be performed during the course of the assignment, with details as to the types of research being proposed and how they will be used to achieve the overall objectives of the engagement

- Secondary source research that will be conducted, with specifics as to the types of information that will be collected

- Interviews that will be conducted by your organization to gather necessary information

- Computer models that will be developed to assist in the analytical part of the assignment

- Group meetings that will allow the consultants involved in the assignment to compare notes on the information that they

have accumulated and to develop appropriate conclusions
and recommendations

In net, you should outline each of the steps of the project implementation so that the prospect organization can get a notion of how you have thought through the assignment.

Section 6. Timing

This section should present an overview of the timing that will be required to complete the assignment, along with any key intermediary dates. The end point should coincide with the client organization's due date, and the intermediary points should be realistic for the consultant. This is very important: Any dates included in a proposal will be considered by the client organization to be sacrosanct, unless there is a very good reason for a change. To this end, the timing should always begin with an assumed start date, so that a client starting the project late will not expect you to complete the work according to timing in the original proposal.

Over the years, I have found it very helpful to include in the proposal a flow chart that shows on one page when each step of the project will be completed. This is developed by listing the various steps of the approach along the left-hand side of the page and the weeks along the top. Then I draw horizontal lines showing when each of the steps starts and ends, so that anyone looking at the chart will get an excellent understanding of how the various phases of the project integrate and when each starts and finishes.

Section 7. Staffing

This portion of the proposal should identify the people in your consulting organization who will make up the project team. In the case of a small organization, it might only be one person or two, or only the consultant and some outside associates who will participate in various phases of the assignment. The keys to the staffing section are to communicate clearly who will be involved in the assignment, to insure that the prospect organization understands the roles of the various people, and to build credibility for the proposal based on the qualifications of the people on the project team.

Section 8. Qualifications

This is the primary selling part of the proposal, as it is where you identify precisely why you feel that you are the best possible consultant for the assignment. You should describe the prior experience of yourself, your consulting company, and your associates in the business for which the proposal is being written and in the functional area for which assistance is desired. You should also mention any other prior experience that is particularly relevant to the work for which the proposal is being developed, as well as any other key information about the consulting company that will further improve your chances of being retained for the assignment.

Section 9. Fees and Expenses

This section should contain the financial aspects of the consulting assignment and would normally include the total fee that you will charge to complete the assignment, the anticipated payment schedule for the consulting fees (i.e., monthly, quarterly, one-third in advance, etc.); and any other expenses incurred in the course of the assignment that will be charged to the client organization, such as the costs of primary or secondary research, travel expenses, long distance telephone charges, express mail/messenger charges, and the costs of presentation materials.

With regard to this section of the plan, it is always best to be as precise as possible. For example, if you need/want to travel first class when you fly, this should be specified in the proposal. If you will be doing research, you need to identify exactly what costs will be incurred and who is responsible for paying them.

Section 10. The Close

This final section of the proposal should state how interested you are in conducting the assignment and should indicate to the prospect contact that if this individual has any questions about the proposal or wishes to make any changes before it is submitted to the entire organization, he should call you to discuss his concerns. It should also run through what you perceive to be the next steps in the process. For example, you might include that you will call the prospect contact in one week to discuss the content of the proposal, just so he knows that he will be hearing from you.

Signature Block

There are many different views regarding how a consulting proposal should be signed, but the one that I personally favor is

For the JAG Consulting Group

Jack A. Green
President

PROPOSAL ISSUES

Charging for Proposals

When I discuss the sales process with a group of consultants or prospective consultants, one question that always arises is whether one can or should charge prospective clients for proposals. This is a very complex issue, and the answer depends on a variety of factors, among them, the standards among the competitive consulting companies, the practices in the industries/companies for whom one is developing a proposal, the definition of a proposal, in terms of how much real consulting one gives away to the prospect organization in the process, and the state of the consultant's business.

In general, most consulting companies do not charge for proposals, as long as they are similar in content to the prototype described in this chapter, in which the only information of any value that the prospect organization receives is the approach to implementing the proposed assignment. However, in some areas of consulting, the consultant must spend considerable time studying the client's business and/or the industry in which the organization is competing in order to develop a meaningful proposal. In this situation, it would be very appropriate to charge a fee for developing the proposal.

Recognizing that the actual practices of charging prospect organizations for proposals differ dramatically by industry, organization, and probably area of the country, perhaps the most helpful thing that this chapter can do is to raise the issues that most people consider when determining whether they will charge for proposals.

Some consultants that charge for proposals indicate that they do so because their time is a very valuable commodity, and so they feel that they should be paid for any work they do for a client or a prospective client. Others feel that if they charge for proposals, only organizations that are very serious about the assignment and therefore represent viable prospects will request them. The consultants argue that, as a result, their time is utilized much more effectively. There are also organizations that believe that the proposal has an inherent value that the prospect could use to its business benefit. Some consultants feel that even the presentation of the approach has definite value to the client, as it tells how the assignment should be handled. Other consultants feel that the receipt of a detailed proposal with a price attached to it also has value to the prospect organization, it can serve as negotiating leverage with other consultants who are bidding for the project.

There are basically two commonly used approaches to charging for a proposal. In the cash approach, the consultant simply establishes a fee and accompanies the proposal with a bill. In these situations, the prospect organization must understand up front that it will be charged for the proposal, whether or not it accepts it. In the credit approach, the consultant informs the prospect organization that it will be credited for the proposal fee in the event that the consultant is selected for the assignment.

The actual amount you charge for a proposal usually is more a function of what you feel you can recover than of any particular economic formula. While you should seek to recover the hourly rate for the time spent researching and developing the proposal, you will almost never succeed, and to come close to breaking even is very acceptable.

The vast majority of consultants, however, do not charge for proposals. Many argue that the absolute value of the proposal is very limited, since the client organization cannot implement the assignment with only an outline of the approach. They further argue that the economic value of a written proposal with a fee attached is limited, since one normally would not use such a document in negotiations with other consulting candidates. Therefore, it would be neither fair nor judicious to charge for a service that has little inherent value to the prospect organization.

Other consultants feel that the absolute number of requests they get to prepare proposals will be dramatically lower if they charge for such documents. Many consulting organizations do not want a policy of charging for proposals to preselect prospective clients before they get to meet them. These consultants feel that they will have a greater chance of building their practices if they develop proposals for all prospective clients than they would if they had to wait around for companies who were willing to pay for proposals. Further, some consultants do not think that they can charge enough for proposals for this to make a meaningful difference in the overall profitability of the business and so do not want to risk the ill will that may be associated with this practice.

Finally, most consultants simply view writing proposals as part of the new business sales effort that any company needs to mount if it is to be successful. Since the activity is viewed as a necessary business expense, it is acceptable not to pass on the costs of the proposal to the prospect organization.

Accounting for Proposal Time

Even if they do not charge prospect organizations for proposals, the better-organized consulting companies will account for this time in one of two ways. Many allocate all costs of bringing in new business to a time category called "New Business Development," which ultimately becomes part of the selling expense for the year, allowing the consultant to calculate how much was spent on this aspect of the business. A second way of accounting for this time is to allocate it to an account that will be activated in the event the organization signs the contract. At that point, the consultant assigns the development costs to the client and recovers them during the first six to twelve months of the assignment. The big problem with this approach is that, in assignments where the consultant must account very tightly for the time spent on the project, he or she will not be able to hide these development costs in the overall expenses.

Responding to Requests for Proposals (RFPs)

Many organizations feel that the most effective way to select a consultant is to develop a detailed specifications document outlining the assignment and then to send this to selected organizations for their response. The scope of these RFPs—requests for proposals—can vary considerably. For example, some users of consulting services such as governmental bodies and industry associations, send out dozens of RFPs (or even more) for each assignment, mailed to specific prescreened organizations or to all organizations on a preestablished mailing list. In other cases, RFPs are published and open to anyone who wishes to respond.

RFPs sometimes contain a cover letter stating that the sponsoring organization is interested in working with the most qualified consultant and that, if the prospective assignment is not within the recipient's area of expertise, it would be appreciated if the consultant would pass it along to others who might be more qualified.

Some organizations use RFPs just to make sure that everyone asked to propose on a particular assignment works with the same general parameters. In these cases, the RFP might go to only a very small number of heavily screened candidate organizations, all of which the client believes to be qualified to do the assignment.

Organizations use RFPs for several reasons. As mentioned, with an RFP, all proposals are based on the same assignment parameters, which makes them much easier to evaluate. RFPs also make it possible for organizations to submit consulting assignments to multiple suppliers, without having to conduct individual briefings.

Some organizations believe that the RFP approach increases their chances of getting the best price for the job, because the candidate organizations know that others are bidding for the job. Still others feel that the RFP process is self-selecting because only consultants that are both qualified to implement the assignment and anxious to work with the sponsor will take the time to respond.

Some consulting companies ignore all RFPs, unless they have a relationship with the sponsoring company and know that the reason for the RFP is to assure equality of proposal content among a selected group of highly qualified consultants. They feel that, except in those circumstances, the probability of being selected for the assignment is very low, because of the likelihood that a large number of RFPs have been distributed and so prefer to spend their time on new business endeavors that have a greater chance of success. Others see the RFP as a sign that the sponsoring organization is shopping around and have no desire to compete on that level. Many feel that the typical RFP requires them to give away more information than the sponsoring organization really needs to select a consultant.

When you must decide whether to respond to a given RFP, ask yourself the following questions.

1. Do the qualifications specified in the RFP match the skills of your organization? If they do not, it probably is a waste of time to respond.

2. How much do you need or want the business? If revenues are coming in slowly (or more slowly than desired) and you have time to develop the requested proposal, it is probably worthwhile to pursue the lead.

3. What effort is involved in developing the proposal? This, too, is a key area. If the proposal will require extensive work to prepare, you must be very sure that it is worth the time. On the other hand, if you can develop the proposal without a major effort, very likely, the work is worthwhile.

4. What is the value of the potential project? This relates to the absolute dollar volume that could be generated in revenues but also to any nonfinancial benefits of the potential assignment, such as adding a prestigious client (or product category) to your client list, having a chance to come into contact with people who may be excellent potential sources of future projects, or gaining some consulting experience in an area that will prove useful later on.

Presenting the Proposal

Once you have developed a proposal, you must figure out the most effective way to present the material to the prospect organization. Should it be mailed, or should you present it in person to the client organization? Several factors affect this decision.

Does the prospect organization want to sit through another meeting in order to have the proposal presented? Some feel it is absolutely necessary so that all questions are addressed immediately to ensure that the content of the proposal is fully understood by all parties. Others prefer not to take the time to have a formal meeting and are more comfortable with a written document.

Where is the client organization located in relation to your offices? If it is in the same town (or very nearby), it is quite feasible to present the document; however, if you would have to spend significant monies to travel to the client location, this might not be a desirable option.

Do you have the time to spare? Although new business is the lifeblood of consulting, often, current clients simply are more important than prospects, and you must spend your available time attending to the present business.

In most cases, presenting a proposal is preferable to mailing it to the client; only you, however, can determine whether it is sufficiently important to justify the additional time and money. Some people feel that all costs incurred to develop the business are sunk, regardless, so they will do whatever it takes to sign the business at this stage, in order to have a chance to recoup their investment. Others present only when it is absolutely necessary and, in most cases, just mail the proposal to the client organization.

Writing Proposals in the Form of Contracts

One of the issues that consultants face is whether they should try to get their clients under contract. Some consultants put an acceptance block at the end of all proposals and will not begin an assignment until the client returns the signed document. Other consulting organizations draw up legal contracts.

Consultants who have their clients sign contracts generally do so because they feel it gives them some legal protection in the event that it is necessary to institute a suit to collect outstanding fees. They also feel that the client signature on the actual document will ensure more commitment from the client organization regarding the nature and scope of the assignment. Those who do not have clients sign contracts feel that this begins a consulting assignment on a basis of trust, which is essential if the relationship is to work out for both organizations. Some have decided never to sue clients (former clients) in the event of nonpayment, because of the trouble and expense that this entails, so any contract would be pointless.

In many situations, the consultant decides not to get the proposal (or a contract) signed but instead writes the client a confirming letter at the time the assignment begins. This, many feel, provides sufficient protection, while avoiding the strains that a contract can place on the client/consultant relationship.

FOLLOW-UP

Once the proposal has been written and exposed to the prospect organization (either by mail or in person), the only thing left is to get the assignment. Thus, the objective of the follow-up is very simple: To close the deal!

Most consultants would agree that the longer the gap between the time the proposal is mailed/presented and the prospect organization's response, the smaller the chances that the proposal will be accepted. Many consulting organizations make the mistake of assuming that any outstanding proposal still may be accepted; however, in most consulting practices, the general feeling is that it is a rare proposal that gets accepted after it has been out of the consultant's office for more than approximately four weeks.

How, then, does the follow-up step help the selling process? First, the follow-up communicates to the prospect organization your interest in the assignment and your desire to work on it. Some consultants never follow up on their proposals, so prospect organizations get the feeling that they are not that interested and do not bother to consider them.

A follow-up also gives you the opportunity to answer any questions that may have surfaced at the prospect organization as a result of your proposal. It is very helpful at this point to clarify any outstanding issues that may be affecting the decision as to which company to hire for the assignment.

By following-up your proposal, you also maintain visibility at the prospect organization, so that your proposal will get the time and attention it needs to be successful. This is particularly helpful when you are bidding against several different consultants.

It should be noted that there are some negatives associated with following up on proposals. Some companies may feel that you are being too pushy. This can be a real turn-off to some organizations and can actually work to the detriment of the consultant. The prospect organization may also see the follow-up as a sign that you are really hurting for business. This, too, can work against you, as few companies want to be associated with a consultant who is not succeeding.

Based on my experience, the best approach to following up consulting proposals is to call up the client approximately two to three days after you mailed your proposal to confirm that it arrived safely. This will give you the opportunity to get some preliminary reaction to your proposal. In some cases, this phone call will tell you whether you have won the assignment; even when it doesn't, it will send a message that you are interested in the prospect's business.

At the time you talk to the prospect contact, it is very appropriate to ask when he or she thinks the company will make a decision about the project. You should call at that time to remind the prospect contact that he or she told you to check back at this time in order to find out who the organization has selected to handle the assignment. In the event there is still no decision, you should ask once more for the best estimate of when the decision is forthcoming and, again, call back at that time. This process can go on for quite a while, depending largely on the decision-making process within the prospect organization.

Unfortunately, there is no real way to know when a proposal is dead, unless the prospect says so outright. However, it usually is time to give up if the prospect contact does not return your telephone calls and is very difficult to reach when you try to call, if the contact appears annoyed when you call, or if he does not suggest that you check back on such and such date.

How to Handle Proposal Negotiating

On occasion, a prospect organization will try to negotiate the contract, usually seeking to reduce the price, expand the scope of the proposal while holding the price constant, or speed up the schedule.

Reducing the price. Generally, it is a very bad policy to reduce the price of a consulting proposal simply because the prospect has suggested such a change. It suggests to the prospect organization that your original price was too high or that the margins you built into the proposal could easily have been trimmed. Moreover, an arbitrary price reduction can come back to haunt you in all future proposal submissions to an organization, as it will assume that it can always negotiate with you for a better fee. It also sends a message to the prospect organization that you are hungry and will do whatever it takes to win an assignment.

It has been my experience that the best way to handle a situation where the client is trying to negotiate price is to indicate that you would be willing to reduce your price, but in order to do so, it will be necessary to cut back on some of the scope of the assignment. This sets a very proper tone, indicating you are sensitive to their cost and budget needs but that your work is worth the price that you charge.

Broadening the scope. Some prospect organizations will attempt to squeeze a little more work out of you, when you both know that you are quite close to a deal. In this situation, you should try to cut back on some other part of the project in order to handle the added work, so that your total time outlay will remain roughly the same. If you do not succeed in this effort, you will have to make a decision regarding how feasible it would be to take on the extra work, given the budget established for the project. This is a hard decision in most cases, but, if the added work is relatively minor, it is generally a good idea to accept it, making it clear to the client that you are doing so in the name of good will, even though it is beyond the scope of what was agreed.

Changing the timing. It is very common for prospect organizations to request that projects be completed before the time indicated in the proposal. Whether you agree to such changes depends mostly on the impact that the tighter deadline will have on other projects already in progress. If you can handle the request without disrupting the overall operations of your consulting organization, you should agree to the new schedule. If, on the other hand, the timing creates problems, you could quite reasonably negotiate for a compromise in the due date or to inform the client that the new timing will result in additional fees.

The entire objective of the follow-up phase of the selling process is to get the business, but not at the expense of your integrity or your profitability. Consultants deserve to make money, too, and prospect organizations need to understand this when evaluating proposals.

SUMMARY

The proposal is the document that actually gets you the business, and, often, it is the only thing that many people in the client organization will see before you are hired for the assignment. It must be viewed as a selling document, and care should be taken to see that it is extremely well written and developed in such a manner that the prospect organization will be sold on your services. In my consulting career, I have seen many excellent salespeople who were able to generate the interest of the prospect organization, only to lose the contract because of a poorly developed proposal. You need effective sales to get you to the proposal stage, but you then need excellent proposal skills to win the contract. It is the one-two punch that determines who is successful in selling consulting services and who is not.

12 Handling Objections

Under ideal circumstances, you would never need to handle objections; you would simply tell your story to the prospect organization, and it would hire you to complete the assignment. Unfortunately, this is rarely the case. In many consulting sales situations, people in the client organization will raise objections that threaten your ability to close the sale. The purpose of this chapter is to discuss the most common objections that prospect organizations raise to consultants and to provide some assistance in answering these objections. Also, this chapter offers some basic guidelines on what you should and should not do in order to turn an objection into a sale.

HANDLING OBJECTIONS—THE BASICS

Like all aspects of selling, most objections can be handled, if the salesperson does a thorough job of planning the response and understands some of the basic techniques for dealing with objections. Many books have been written about the most effective ways to handle objections in selling situations. This section is not meant as a substitute for the material in those books, nor do I pretend to have found a way to simplify a very difficult subject. Rather, my intent is to share some basic techniques that should help the person selling consulting services to get past the initial "no."

Principle 1. Understand That a "No" Does Not Necessarily Mean "No"

Too often in a selling situation, a consultant will stop a presentation as soon as the client contact says "no" or something very close to "no." In fact, "no" can mean many different things, among them "no," "not at this time," "I would like to do it but do not have the money," "my boss would never approve of this because it is not a budgeted expense." One should always consider the first (and probably the second and third) "no" to be more a request for information than a rejection of the idea. In many cases a way around the "no" is to provide additional information that will lead the client to the all-important "yes."

Principle 2. Know When a "No" Does Mean "No"

The idea that the word "no" is simply a signpost on the road to "yes" is so ingrained in many salespeople that they often forget that it can be the terminal response. The most effective salespeople have an instinct for sensing when the "no" really is a "no" and it is time to walk away from the selling situation and spend time on other prospects who may say "yes."

Unfortunately, a great deal of the talent for knowing when "no" really means "no" comes from instinct and the ability to read nonverbal messages (i.e., a look of boredom, checking their watches, arms folded in front, yawning, roving eyes, etc.). Still, there are a few pointers that can often help the consultant know when it is time to back off.

1. The recognition that the prospect has not changed his or her position toward your service, regardless of how you have handled various objections.

2. The sense that the prospect is becoming annoyed with you during the presentation.

3. A lack of response after you have tried a different approach toward achieving a close.

Principle 3. Do Not Get Emotional

One of the most destructive things a salesperson can do is to become emotional when the prospect raises an objection. Generally, this only makes the prospect more fixed in his or her position. Further, when you become emotional in this situation, it often sends a message that you are unsure of what you are selling or that the prospect's point is particularly sensitive (i.e., good).

Principle 4. Repeat the Objection

One of the most important things that a salesperson can do is to repeat an objection that has been raised. This forces the prospect to think over the objection to ensure that it is accurate. Sometimes, when prospects hear a point repeated, they realize that it is not what they meant to say. The repetition also assures that both parties in the transaction fully understand the objection, so that, when you begin the process of overcoming it, nothing will be omitted.

Principle 5. Prepare to Handle Objections

Most objections stem (in some way) from lack of money, lack of need, lack of time, or insecurity about hiring a consultant. The effective salesperson will develop (in writing) a list of the most common objections, attributing each to the appropriate motivation, and then write a brief response to each, indicating the most important points that should be raised when a prospect brings one of them up. The best salespeople keep notebooks in which they summarize each objection as it arises, the points that should be used to combat it, and what they used and how it worked. If you follow this practice, you soon will have a databank of information, which will become second nature to you, that you can use the next time you must handle an objection.

Principle 6. Handle Every Objection Precisely When It Is Raised

Some salespeople make the mistake of feeling compelled to finish their sales presentations before they handle objections. This is very destructive and, in fact, counterproductive. Once an objection has been raised, it will stay on the prospect's mind until it is answered; it is highly unlikely that the prospect will be able to pay attention to the rest of the presentation. Also, if you wait to handle objections, you give the impression that you think neither the prospect's opinion nor the objection is important. Needless to say, this can have a very detrimental effect on the relationship.

Another reason to handle objections as soon as they come up is that you could easily forget to deal with some of them at the end, and the prospect could walk away from the presentation feeling that one of his greatest concerns was not addressed.

Finally, if you try to handle all objections at the end of a presentation, you have to win a series of battles in a row in order to win the war. This is very difficult; your natural inclination will be to compromise, and this may not be possible if you are to make the sale. In any case, you may have to leave the presentation on a negative note, rather than on the positive high that is conducive to generating a close.

Principle 7. Handle Objections Piece by Piece

One of the most effective ways to handle objections is to deal with each part of an objection in as small a parcel as possible. If you deal with each part to the satisfaction of the prospect, the probability of gaining the right to proceed with the presentation will be much greater.

Principle 8. Get Permission to Proceed

You should never consider an objection resolved until the prospect indicates that it is time to proceed with the presentation. Only at that point can you be sure that the prospect is satisfied with your responses to his or her concerns.

Principle 9. Do Not Give Up

If you are not successful in eliminating an objection, the probability of your closing the sale will be significantly reduced. Therefore, when you encounter an objection, keep trying until you overcome it, even if this requires you to use several different approaches.

Principle 10. When You Succeed, Run Like Hell

This is a very good general principle of selling: When you get the order, move on, since, presumably, that was the purpose of the sales call. The same is true of handling objections. When you overcome an objection, move away from that point immediately and continue with the balance of the presentation. You do not want the prospect to revisit the objection, nor do you want to give any more information that might change his or her mind.

HANDLING OBJECTIONS—THE GENERIC RESISTANCE TO CONSULTANTS

Consulting services are among the most difficult products in the world to sell. This section will discuss several reasons for this and provide some thoughts on how to overcome each of these obstacles to the sales process.

Objection 1. You Are Selling an Intangible

Most consulting services consist of little more than the brainpower, talent, and experience of the people in the organization. These are much more difficult to sell than an automobile, a suit, or a computer program, which are tangibles that the purchaser can see, feel, and actually experience. The end product of a consulting assignment is often a report or simply a set of recommendations; there is no way for the purchaser to evaluate it until it has been delivered.

The intangible nature of consulting services clearly is one of the most difficult objections to handle. However, some consultants neutralize this point simply by making their intangible service tangible, usually by packaging some or all of their services into a product that has a name, an identity, and, possibly, its own marketing plan. Suppose you operate a human resource business aimed at assisting clients in evaluating employees for hiring. Your service includes an initial interview, a follow-up test for those who pass the first round, an analysis of the test, a background check on people who pass, and a write-up of your recommendation. Now, suppose that, instead of offering yourself as a professional resource to help clients with the hiring process you can offer them a product, called, say, PeopleScope, which you sell as an independent "product." You have made an intangible into a tangible, simply by naming it, promoting it, and selling it as if it were a tangible.

Objection 2. You Are Selling without a Guarantee

Most consulting services are provided on a best-effort basis, where the consultant comes into the client organization, analyzes the situation, and then submits a report that includes recommendations that the consultant believes will solve the problem. In many ways, the client is in the same position as a doctor's patient: Both are required to pay a fee even if their problems are not solved. Both doctor and consultant furnish their recommendations in good faith. Sometimes, they do not work, and, frequently, this is due more to inadequate implementation of the proposed solution than to improperly developed recommendations.

What can you do to sell effectively when a prospect is looking for a guarantee? An obvious answer is to offer some sort of money-back guarantee in the event the client is not satisfied with the work. I do *not* favor this approach. First, it gives the client the option not to pay, even if your work was excellent. When organizations undergo difficult times, they sometimes delay (or avoid) paying smaller suppliers. You do not want to give such clients an excuse not to pay. Second, sometimes the ultimate success of a consulting assignment is not under your control. Outside factors can come into play that might take your very good effort and make the solution not work. And, third, it can give the impression that you are very hungry for business and will do anything to add clients to your list. This is not an impression that you want to foster.

If providing a guarantee is not the answer, then what is? I have found two very effective ways to handle this situation, which make clients feel that they have got a guarantee but involve no actual agreement to that effect on your part.

Your first course is to indicate to your clients that you would not consider any assignment complete until they are perfectly happy with the work. I believe, in fact, that most consultants should take this position almost 100 percent of the time. The client's happiness and satisfaction with the work that is accomplished is vital to a successful consulting relationship; this, in essence, is what the prospect hopes a guarantee will assure.

The second approach is to cite similar assignments that you have handled in the past in order to show prospects that you know how to address their situations. You want to communicate an air of confidence, so that the prospect feels that your experience constitutes a guarantee.

Objection 3. You Are Often Selling to a Poorly Defined Need

In many cases, the consultant is brought into a situation where the client needs a solution to a problem that has not been clearly identified. Say, for example, that a company is considering hiring a human resources consultant to fix a major problem with employee morale, the cause of which has yet to be defined. You, the consultant, must determine whether the problem is a function of poor personnel policies, the management structure, compensation, working conditions or whatever, before you can begin to create solutions. The nature and scope of the entire consulting assignment will depend largely on what you identify to be the problem. This lack of a clear definition of the scope of the consulting assignment makes it very difficult for the consultant to develop a proposal that will convince the prospective client to allocate corporate funds to fix the problem.

In this type of situation, your natural inclination will be to tell the client that the project is poorly defined and then set out to demonstrate your analytical capabilities and problem-solving skills. This approach, however, can work to your disadvantage, since it may start your relationship with the client on an adversarial basis. A better approach is to seek to direct the conversation in a way that will lead the client contact to conclude for him- or herself that additional work needs to be done to define the problem properly. This is relatively simple to accomplish during the first interview with the client prospect. Specifically, when you realize that the problem is complex, immediately ask the client contact what he or she believes to be the principal causes of the problem. Your ostensible motive for the question should be to gain background information that will enable you to write a more effective proposal. If this interview is handled well, the prospective client will begin to realize that there are many different possible causes of the problem and that, before any programs for resolution can be developed, it will be necessary to define the project objectives and scope more clearly. The key is for the prospect to come to this conclusion, not you.

This approach makes the client contact feel good because he or she is the one that decides how to proceed with the consulting assignment. The client will feel that he or she is directing the consultant, rather than being told what to do all the time. The working relationship thus begins on a much better footing. Your proposal will already have the buy-in of the prospect and its scope (and perhaps even the costs and timing) will not be as much of a surprise as it would be if the foundation of the initial relationship were different.

Objection 4. You Are Selling in a Very Competitive Environment

The consulting business is one of today's most competitive industries. More and more people have identified consulting as a career choice for themselves, either because they inherently like the work, want the lifestyle or prestige associated with it, or, in a larger percentage of the cases, because of an absence of other job opportunities. The cost of entering the field is extremely low, and there are no licensing requirements for entry into virtually all aspects of consulting. As a result, it is very common for out-of-work executives, retired professionals, or members of the academic community to offer their services as consultants in their areas of expertise. With the large number of consultants in most fields, clients are more likely than ever before to talk to several different organizations about potential assignments, in order to identify the one group (or individual) that will offer the optimal mix or price capabilities. The impact of this on the consulting industry is that price has become a much more important factor in selecting a consulting organization than it has been in the past, and client organizations feel that they have considerable bargaining power with the various organizations competing to service their needs.

I feel there are three key things that you can do to sell effectively in a very competitive market. First, you must fully understand what criteria the prospect organization is using in its selection process. Is it seeking

- technical expertise in a very specialized area?
- an evaluation by a prestigious third-party organization to help sell a point of view internally (i.e., to the Board)?
- relatively inexpensive extra help in getting through a particularly difficult period?

- hands-on help in managing a part of the business for a short period of time?

- in-depth analytical assistance to solve very complex problems of a significant magnitude?

By identifying the prospect's motives for hiring a consultant, you can stress those strengths that relate most to the prospect's needs.

Second, you should try to determine the nature of your competition. Often, the client will be willing to tell you about this, sometimes going so far as to reveal the names of specific competitors. Some consultants are reluctant to ask for this kind of information, but the more you know about the organizations with which you are competing, the better prepared you will be to sell for yourself and against them. For example, if you operate a one-person consulting organization, your selling strategy would differ depending on whether the competition were other one-person consulting groups, part-time professors from the local university, the consulting division of a large accounting firm, a medium-size consulting group that specializes in this area of the profession, a large management consulting firm, or a relative of the key client contact.

Third, you should evaluate your company's strengths in light of the above so that you can develop a very strong sales approach emphasizing those that coincide most with the prospect organization's needs without being critical or negative toward the competition.

Some people feel that when they get into heavily competitive situations, they must reduce the price of their services to win the business. I feel strongly, however, that you should not use pricing as a selling mechanism. For one thing, normally, it will not work. Most people buying consulting services are concerned with price, but usually not to the point where it will be a major factor in the decision. This is not to suggest that your price should not be competitive, but rather that you should not cut your prices specifically to get an assignment.

The most important reason for not dropping your price in the sales process relates to the opportunity revenues that would be lost by such an approach. I have seen many situations where consultants in need of business have decided to reduce their prices significantly in order to bring new assignments in the door. Often, they fill their time with low-profit work and, consequently, are unable to accept other more profitable work when it comes along. They frequently begin to resent these projects and have difficulty doing their best work because of the anger that builds up.

The end result is an unsatisfactory consulting engagement for which they have been paid less than an acceptable fee.

A final argument against using price to get an assignment is that it often makes it very difficult for you to revert to your regular pricing schedule the next time you bid for an assignment from this client.

If pricing is an important issue with the prospect organization, I have found that the most effective approach to sell the prospect on a phased assignment. For example, if you calculate that the entire assignment might cost $100,000, you could break the project into two (or maybe even more) phases, in order to get the absolute cost per phase down to a level that is more acceptable to the client. Maybe the initial phase of the project could be accomplished for $30,000, and the contract would not obligate the prospect organization to the second phase. Often, this type of arrangement suits both parties, as the consultant get the full revenue for the work that is accomplished and the client organization gets assistance at a price that it can afford. Further, if the output of the first phase is well done and effectively presented, there is usually no problem getting the client to agree to the second phase.

Objection 5. There Are Many "No" People and Few "Yes" People

Most consultants have had the experience of making a presentation to a prospective client, only to find out that the people to whom they are presenting do not have the authority to hire them, but only the authority to say "no." Often, you will be faced with the difficult task of having to sell to intermediaries who may or may not give you an opportunity to meet with the decision makers in the organization.

To improve your chances of success in these situations, you should do as much research as possible on the prospect organization, in order to find out who its "yes" people are. The obvious goal here is to avoid presenting (if at all possible) unless the decision maker is present. Unfortunately, however, you often will have to present to an intermediary first. In these cases, your objective is to convince the intermediary that it is in his or her best interests to hire you, as this will work to the intermediary's personal advantage over time. In essence, you want this individual to become your advocate, the one who carries your flag to the decision makers in the organization. There are some important things that you can do to improve the chances of a successful sale in this situation.

1. Demonstrate how your involvement with the client organization will be good for the intermediary who is responsible for hiring you. You might cite other similar occasions when your client contacts received promotions, raises, or simply a great deal of praise because they were smart enough to recognize the need for an outside organization.

2. Emphasize that your objective is to stay in the background and make the client contact look good. Make it clear that you are not trying to make the contact look bad, or even steal the thunder associated with the consulting program, but rather that you exist to serve the contract effectively so that he or she achieves objectives.

3. Make it easy for the intermediary to sell your services to the organization. This is the point where so many consultants lose sight of the selling chain that exists in many organizations. They may make a very successful presentation to the intermediary and then wonder why they got turned down when the project was exposed to the higher-ups in the organization. In many cases, the fault lies with the consulting salesperson, not the intermediary, because the consultant did not do one or two very important things.

   First, the consultant did not make an effective case for the intermediary to set up a meeting with the decision makers. This is usually the best way to sell a proposal to the people with "yes" authority, as the consultant is in a much better position to sell his or her services than would be an individual who is not very familiar with the consultant's company and capabilities.

   Second, the consultant salesperson did not prepare the intermediary effectively to sell the project. Once control of the sell-in process falls into the hands of a third party, the consultant must ensure that this person is capable of selling the service, or all the time spent up to this point will be wasted. To this end, the consultant can provide the intermediary with sufficient information so that he or she can make an effective presentation. Normally, this information should include such things as

- a presentation outline to be used with the prospect organization decision makers. This outline should follow essentially the same format as that used by the consultant initially to sell to the intermediary.

- a briefing document that lists the key objections that the intermediary is likely to encounter and summarizes how each objection should be handled

- information about the consulting company, which the intermediary can provide to the people in attendance so that they can learn about the consultant's experience and overall capabilities

The consultant should make sure that the prospect contact fully understands these materials and is comfortable using them. It is particularly important for the consultant to impress on the prospect contact the importance of presenting the case as the consultant has prepared it, so that the full story gets communicated in an effective and convincing manner.

Finally, the consultant should be available before the meeting, to answer any last-minute questions that arise, as the contact begins to review the materials provided in the preparation for the presentation, and immediately afterward to answer questions that are raised about the prospective assignment.

In some cases, you will be asked to attend the meeting, but only as an observer, while the prospect contact presents the materials. This is a difficult position for most consultants, as they know others will not be able to present their cases as well as they can and to watch this happen is even more painful. However, it is strongly recommended that you attend and participate only when asked—this will reinforce your relationship with the prospect contact and demonstrate that you are there to support him, not to take the credit.

Objection 6. Many Client Personnel Feel Threatened by Consultants

People whom you are trying to convince to purchase your service may be afraid of hiring you. Rather than recognizing that there are some areas where they (or the organization) do not have the expertise or the objectivity to solve a particular problem, some people simply shy away from employing consultants and try to solve the problems internally. One or more of the following may be responsible for this.

Concerns about individual competency. People in client organizations may be concerned that hiring a consultant to assist in a particular project will make them look bad, because they believe that management expects them to have the skills that the consultant possesses.

Concerns about job security. These people may be concerned the consultant will come into the company and determine that they are not competent. This is a great fear among many client contacts, as consultants have a reputation in many fields for being the catalyst for personnel and organizational changes.

Concerns about budgets. Some people in client organizations are more concerned with meeting their expense budgets than their business goals, and they have great difficulty dealing with the costs of a consultant, given that the results of their work may be longer term in nature.

Concerns about losing control. Finally, some people feel that the control over the project and its related areas will be lost to the consultant. As a result, they think that their power base within the company will be reduced, which has an immediate effect of deflating their personal sense of worth.

There are a few techniques that normally will alleviate some, if not all, of the concerns in this area. First, you should emphasize that your principal objective in the engagement is to achieve the specific mission that has been assigned. You should point out that a consulting organization builds its business from happy client personnel who will refer the organization to others. Therefore, the execution of any assignment is geared toward achieving the objectives, while, at the same time, ensuring that the client personnel are happy.

Second, you should inform the client contact of the frequency with which the person in that position ends up with additional responsibility or a promotion as a direct result of consultant involvement. The aim here is to point out that senior management is primarily interested in achieving the established objectives, and not in how this gets done. It is much better to retain a consultant and achieve the objectives than it is to refrain from bringing in an outsider and fail to achieve them.

Third, you should provide the client contact with an overview of the process that you use to work with a client. The objectives here are threefold:

1. To demonstrate that the approval authority lies in the contact's hands. In essence, the key is to point out that the prospect is the client—the boss.

2. To communicate that you do not want the limelight—it is reserved for the prospect contact. The role of the consultant is to provide the prospect contact with information so that he or she can look good within the organization for having hired the consultant.

3. To show how the prospect contact will be involved with your organization throughout the assignment, to reinforce the fact that the prospect will not lose control over the project when he or she retains a consultant.

Sometimes, it is impossible to convince a prospect contact that you will not be a threat to him in some way; however, following the pointers in this section should minimize the problem so that it does not get in the way of closing the sale.

Objection 7. Many People Feel that They Are Experts and Do Not Need Consulting Assistance

This objection category is one of the more difficult to handle effectively, as it can impact directly on the egos of some client personnel. Suppose you were seeking to convince a prospect that your company could help him develop a more effective marketing program, yet he considers himself a highly talented marketing person who really does not need help. In a situation like this, there are a couple of things you definitely should not do.

These are two principal should-nots. First, never try to prove that the person is not particularly capable by virtue of the lack of success of the business in which you are currently proposing involvement. Often, this is the most obvious approach, since you may be talking to a person who manages a business that has been experiencing steady business losses (or simply negative gains), and your instinct is to indicate to this person, that if he were so good, the business would not be failing or not growing. But, while the lack of growth in the business may be a perfect explanation of why he needs your assistance, to point this out would win you the battle but lose you the war. The prospect might agree with you but probably would not hire you, because you have directly attacked his competence and threatened his self-esteem.

Furthermore, do not try to demonstrate that you have more technical competence in this particular area than he does. To do so would place you in a superior role to the prospect contact, which normally will not result in a successful relationship. He needs to retain his self-esteem and feeling of professionalism and, importantly, the control over any consultant the he hires. To point out your superior skills would destroy this and probably preclude the possibility of a consulting relationship.

Luckily, there are some positive ways to handle this type of situation that will allow you to deal effectively with the prospect's needs, enabling you to sign the contract.

First, you should minimize the technical expertise you bring to the situation and focus instead on the breadth of experience you have had in similar projects. In my experience, people can deal much better with the realization that a consultant can help them because they have seen the problem before in other companies than they can accept the notion of any inherent superiority of skills or intellect.

A second approach is to emphasize that one of the reasons why you can be so helpful is that you can work on the problem full-time, whereas the prospect has to run the rest of the business and cannot focus solely on this issue. This allows the prospect to rationalize the hiring of the consultant in terms of time, instead of asking him to acknowledge his own lack of skills. This much more palatable approach enables the prospect to overcome the psychological problems associated with bringing in an outside expert to solve an internal problem.

Objection 8. Many People Believe that Only Experts in Their Business Can Help

In the 16 years I have been in the consulting business, this has probably been the objection I have had to field the most from prospective clients. In almost every new prospect briefing, you can count on someone in the client organization telling you how different his or her business is from all others and how you need to have specific expertise in its workings to be an effective consultant. These people tend to hire only consultants that have worked in their particular product category or industry many times in the past or refrain from using consultants altogether.

I have not found this common objection difficult to overcome in most situations. Often, it is helpful to observe that, while you recognize that there are certain differences in the company, industry, and product line that make it unique, your experience has shown that all (or virtually all) businesses have some very basic things in common, which enable consultants to be successful without being expert in every aspect of their clients' businesses. In essence, you want to point out that, when you develop your recommendations, you are dealing with principles and processes rather than specific nuances of the business. You should indicate that one of the things you learn as a consultant is to ask the right questions and study the right documents and numbers so that you can become familiar with new business situations very quickly. You should point out that you could not be a successful consultant if you did not know how to become well-educated in your client's business very quickly. This should be done diplomatically, however, as it is often a difficult thing for many client personnel to accept. Point out that your objective is not to become as much of a technical expert in their business as they are, but rather to learn as much as is necessary to enable you to develop effective solutions to their problems. Further, you should mention that you always have them to provide you with technical information during the course of the consulting assignment.

To buttress the prospect organization's confidence in you, you might provide several examples of other consulting assignments where you had no experience in the product category before being hired but quickly were able to develop effective solutions. You also might tell the prospect organization about other consulting assignments where you dealt with the same functional problem, even if it was in a different industry. For example, if the prospect organization is having trouble motivating its sales force, you might give some examples of how you have developed programs in other industries to help clients motivate their selling organizations. This will give you immediate credibility with the prospect organization.

You should not be defensive about not having extensive experience in a specific business when pursuing a consulting assignment. If you have a firm grounding in the principles of your field and have mastered the art of learning a client business quickly, you should be able to enter new situations with great confidence and an attitude that communicates to the prospect organization that you can help it.

Objection 9. Most Client Personnel Have No Notion of What It Costs to Hire a Consultant

You will not be in the consulting business for very long before you first encounter a prospective client who complains rather vociferously at the price you have quoted for a consulting assignment. Usually, these complaints derive from one of the following misapprehensions.

First, most people do not have any conception of what it takes to complete most consulting assignments, in terms of either time or actual cost. The typical new client contact might think that a consultant can finish an assignment in only a few days and that the daily cost for the services should be about $500, thus arriving at a cost that is way off the mark. When the consultant comes back with a cost for the assignment that is many times higher than the estimate, the problems begin.

Second, clients often think of a consultant's fee as an extra, generally neglecting to consider the relative costs of hiring a consultant versus using internal people to do the assignment. If they stopped to figure out what the cost would be to do the job in-house, often the consultant turns out not to be significantly more expensive, because company employees all have costs associated with them (normally, equal to or twice the amount of base salaries). Few client organizations, however, bother to calculate the fully loaded costs that go along with using their own people to complete an assignment. Further, a consultant usually can complete the work in much less time because of expertise in the area and total focus on the project. As a result, clients probably should count each consulting day as about one-and-a-half internal days (on a fully loaded cost basis) to obtain a valid comparison of the costs.

Finally, let's assume you charge a daily rate of $1200, which is average for many types of consulting. Some clients will multiply this daily fee by 360 (yes, a full year, rather than a working year) and conclude that you are making almost $450,000 per year. Even the client contact who multiples the daily rate by 200 (more representative of working days) will feel that you are earning an enormous amount—$240,000 per year—particularly since he or she probably earns dramatically less than that sum. The initial reaction is that you could not possibly be worth five to ten times more than he or she is, and therefore you must be charging exorbitant fees. These clients fail to appreciate the fact that a consultant does not bill 100 percent of the time every day and that, depending on the nature of the consulting business, there can be significant expenses associated with operating the practice.

What, then, can you do to counter an argument over price? A cardinal rule of the consulting business is not to apologize for your pricing schedule. Develop a fee structure that represents fair value for the services you provide and then stick to it. You should never get into a discussion that causes you to justify your rates. You also should never negotiate on rates. You should not have a rate schedule from which you stray in order to obtain different assignments. Price an assignment at the correct value, and, if pricing becomes an issue, reduce costs by cutting out certain aspects of the project (e.g., the depth of research that is implemented, the type of final report that is provided, etc.) rather than offering to do the original assignment for a lower price. As I have said before, if you get the reputation for negotiating fees, clients will assume that you build fat into your estimates and therefore negotiate in order to get what they think is a fair price.

I have found that it is desirable to deal with the pricing issue by informing the client of the methodology you used to arrive at the fee. A detailed proposal often will be an effective document to demonstrate the fairness of your pricing. By identifying the various elements that go into the price you have quoted, you can give the prospect the option of eliminating some parts of the project in order to reduce the costs.

One approach I have used very successfully to avoid pricing issues with clients is to ask them to identify a budget figure for outside consulting services, so that I can identify what I can do for them within that budget. Unfortunately, most people faced with this choice feel that it represents an attempt to maximize income from the assignment and will bulk up the project to absorb the entire budget. They seem convinced that any budget figure they cite will be too high and that, if one develops a proposal without that number, they feel one inevitably will charge less. The reality of this situation is that, in the sixteen years I have been in the consulting business, I have never known a consultant to develop a project fee that was less than the client anticipated—with or without an initial budget.

If you can get the prospect organization to buy into this approach up front, however, it is very helpful and extremely practical. First, it allows you to develop a proposal very efficiently. If you know the total monies you have to complete the assignment, you can work to that amount rather than develop a document that is so comprehensive that it goes well beyond what the client can afford. In other words, you can approach the prospect organization at the outset with a proposal that provides a way to solve its problem within a cost structure that is acceptable. You also have the option of returning to the client with the information that you cannot complete the assignment for the specified amount. Over the years, I have been very successful in situations where we had to go back to prospect organizations for additional monies.

Second, if the prospect organization develops a budget for the prospective assignment, you get a psychological buy-in to the project even before you have developed your proposal. In effect, by giving you the budget, the prospect says that it is prepared to spend that amount of money on your services if the proposal you generate is reasonable.

Finally, this approach enables you to close the assignment much more quickly than would an open-ended pricing effort, because, once the proposal is written, the only issue is whether the prospect feels you are the right person/organization to do the work. Price has been set aside as a given and generally will not become a subject for further discussion. If you use an open-ended approach, on the other hand, it is likely that you will be required to rewrite the proposal at least once because of budget issues.

SUMMARY

Handling objections is as much a science as an art. While some people are much better than others at this facet of selling, some general principles can dramatically improve anyone's performance. The real key to handling objections is to anticipate what obstacles a prospect is likely to put in your way and to plan the most appropriate way to meet them. If you follow this approach, you will find that objections will become less of a problem for you—indeed, they will often become the means whereby you win the contract over the competition.

13 Service in a Consulting Business

Consulting is a service business! If you ever lose sight of that fact, your practice will be sure to suffer. If you can offer a quality product, the service component of your practice will prove to be a very important asset that will contribute significantly to the growth of your business.

What, then, is service as applied to a consulting practice? To answer this question, it is better to begin by establishing what it is not, as the concept of service in a consulting environment is quite different from that in many other types of business. For example, in consulting, service is not based on the principle that the customer is always right. Many consultants have made the mistake of believing that the best way to serve their clients is to provide them with information that agrees with what they want to hear. Others think that they should always give into the client when a dispute emerges about a specific point, since this will be much more beneficial to the long-term relationship with the client organization.

The guideline I have followed for over fifteen years and have preached continually in the courses I have taught is that a consultant is obligated to tell the client what is right for the business, even if this will damage the long-term client-consultant relationship, just as a physician must tell a patient that he has a dreaded disease, recognizing that this will be very

201

painful for both doctor and patient but is in the best interest of both parties to know.

Service in the consulting business also is not providing tickets to theater and sporting events, wining and dining clients, and offering gifts to key client personnel at appropriate times. Some people in the consulting business feel that the way to develop a strong practice is to provide clients with many different types of perks, so that they will feel committed to their consulting organizations. While some client entertainment is likely to be a reasonable (or perhaps necessary) part of any relationship, it should be a very minor element, rather than a key ingredient of a service marketing effort. The major reasons for this are that

- A focus on tickets, dinners, and gifts is very demeaning to the consultant's position and hinders the individual's ability to work as an objective advisor to the client organization.

- The strength of the relationship becomes based on the wrong things, as quality of product becomes secondary to the next perk that will be offered. As a result, the relationship will be threatened by the next person who comes along who is willing to spend more money on these items than the present consultant.

- The type of person who typically is successful in the consulting business is generally more interested in the intellectual/ business-building aspects of the relationship than in wining and dining client personnel.

THE KEY COMPONENTS OF SERVICE

The concept of service varies considerably with the type of consulting practice and even with the nature of the relationship with the client. This section of the book discusses the various components of service and the factors that consultants should consider when determining the extent of the service relationship that they wish to provide.

Personal Involvement with Key Client Personnel

In many assignments, it is very easy for a consultant to attend the first meeting (or meetings) in order to gather the necessary information and then not to make contact with the client organization for several months, perhaps only when the project is completed, to present the final report. This is generally not an effective way to service a client organization, nor is it a good way to develop meaningful relationships with clients that will lead to future assignments.

You should maintain regular contact with the key people in the client organization. The actual frequency of communication and the nature of the contact will differ according to type of assignment and the people in the organization. To meet or at least make telephone contact with the client organization on a weekly basis would not be unusual and, for some organizations (or assignments), would not be enough.

You should also establish a relationship with the key contacts in the client organization, so that they will call you in when they need information or personal contact. This way, the entire burden of keeping in contact will not rest on your shoulders.

Finally, you should visit the client organization whenever it is important. For example, if you attend a meeting on one aspect of the assignment, this is a good time to spend a few minutes meeting with others involved in the project in order to update them on the status of the project and inform them of the plans for the next several days. If this is done regularly, it can be a very important part of the whole service relationship, at the cost of very little extra time or effort.

Availability to Clients

This is a vital aspect of the service mix that you offer your clients, and it involves several different key elements.

The amount of time that you should spend on the client premises. This is a very important issue, which is handled very differently by various consulting companies. Some of the largest consulting companies deal with client service by working at the client premises until the assignment is completed. The rationale for this type of arrangement is that it provides excellent visibility for the consulting organization, both in terms of the specific assignment and to identify future work with the client when the current project is complete. It also places the consultant(s) near the source of much (if not most) of the information required to complete the project, thus making more effective use of the consultant personnel, and enables the consultants to understand the client organization better, because of the closeness that they develop with personnel by being on the premises. Finally, it provides for total availability to the client personnel, since there will almost always be someone from the consultant's organization to help with a specific situation.

There are, however, many consultants who oppose very strongly the idea of working at the client's premises. They do not feel that they can be as efficient when they work at the client organization, because of the distractions of client personnel constantly coming to them for information, much of which is often unrelated to the specific assignment. They also feel that they cannot be as effective in these circumstances. Many consultants find that the key to the quality of their product is the inputs from others in their organization who have had similar experiences in different client situations. When the consultant seeking the information is working away from his or her own offices, he or she will find it is much more difficult to benefit from these experiences.

Many consultants believe that their objectivity and perspective are affected if they work from the clients' premises and have regular involvement with their internal politics. They find it more difficult to make the hard decisions that require them to have some mental distance from the client organization.

The extent to which you should be available to the client, both during and after working hours.   This is a very crucial aspect of the service that you offer to client organizations. If you do not operate your practice on the client's premises, one issue that will continually be a factor is your availability to the client during working hours. You must be willing to juggle schedules to be available when your clients need you. Assuming that you are carrying a reasonable workload, you frequently should be able to change meetings to meet the needs of a specific client situation. If you do not do this, the client can get the impression that other clients are more important to you than they are.

You should also return telephone calls on a timely basis, whether or not you are in your office. Effective service involves being available to the client wherever you are, and this requires you to stay in regular touch with your office throughout the day when you are out, so that clients know you will get back to them within a reasonable period of time.

This situation occasionally raises concerns among some client personnel, who question why their consultant is telephoning another client while in their offices. The best way to respond to this is to remind them that they expect the same when you are at other client offices. Naturally, you want to use discretion regarding both the amount of time you spend on these calls and their frequency; however, they do represent an important component of your service mix.

New communications vehicles, such a beepers and cellular telephones, have enabled some consultants to become even more available to clients. For consultants who spend considerable time in their cars or in locations where access to telephones is not easy, these devices can be extremely helpful.

The entire concept of being available to clients outside of normal working hours is very controversial within the consulting community. Some consultants feel that the service they offer is limited to the normal workday, whereas others are willing to be available to their clients 24 hours a day, seven days a week. The decision is very personal and must be consistent with the needs of the individuals within the consulting organization. I make myself available to clients on an unlimited basis, recognizing that the only time they contact me at unusual times is when a real emergency requires my attention. Only two clients in the past 15 years have abused the privilege of unlimited access to my services at home.

Responsiveness to the Needs of the Client Organization

One of the most important dimensions of customer service is the commitment to being responsive to the needs of your clients. This commitment involves reliability and reactiveness.

You must deliver the completed project to the client organization on time and in the format that was agreed upon in the initial contract. It is very difficult to overestimate the importance of reliability regarding a client-consultant relationship. As an indication of how clients feel about it, one of the strongest reasons some organizations give for using outside consultants is that they are confident that the consultant will deliver, whereas, if the assignment were handled in-house, they would have questions about whether the work would get done.

You must also respond to client requests or suggestions seriously and on a timely basis. For example, if your client suggested that it would be useful to talk to the people in the San Francisco office before you formulate any conclusions, you should decide very quickly whether you need to talk to these people and inform the client of your plan of action. Some clients feel very slighted when consultants ignore their suggestions. You need not accept them all, but at least you should take the time to consider them and respond promptly to the client.

ESTABLISHMENT OF A SERVICE CULTURE

New consultants often ask what approach they should take to developing a commitment to service in their organizations that will become a permanent part of the company culture. I feel there are essentially four things one must do to accomplish this within a consulting practice. Each one is basic to the overall objective to maintaining a major corporate commitment to superior customer service.

Developing a Service Strategy

The first step in the process of building a service culture is to create a brief mission statement outlining the overall objectives of the organization relative to customer service and the specific goals for all aspects of the practice that relate to serving customers. At a minimum, a customer service strategy should stress the importance of the client to the consulting practice, a commitment to meeting deadlines, the importance of building effective relationships with client personnel, the need for responsiveness in all aspects of the business, the importance of integrity and objectivity in customer service, and the need for all people in the organization to be committed to customer service, whether or not they have direct contact with the clients.

Adopting the Service Strategy

Often, senior management creates a statement of the service strategy for the organization and simply sends it out to the employees as a directive, expecting that everyone will immediately adopt the program. This approach rarely works; employees need to feel a part of the program and fully understand their roles before they can (or will) participate. It is necessary to explain to all the people in the organization the nature of the service program that is being adopted and why it is vital for them to contribute to the effort. For example, the people answering telephones need to understand how a friendly telephone voice and effective telephone techniques affect the overall impression that a client or prospect receives regarding the organization. Similar observations can be made of the people in the accounting department or any other group that has contact with personnel in client organizations. Each of these people needs to appreciate the importance of the client and how the overall corporate service strategy affects the way they should do their work every day.

Leading by Example

There are few areas where the benefits of leading by example are more obvious than in customer service. If employees see that the leader(s) of the organization are committed to customer service and they understand what is expected of them in this area, they usually will follow along with the program. On the other hand, if they sense that the customer service commitment is only a lip service mandate from top management, and if they observe the leaders violating their own principles, a program aimed at building customer service in the organization is destined to fail.

Measuring Customer Service Effectiveness

Very few people in service businesses ever take the time to measure their organization's performance in customer service. They assume that the customer service provided is satisfactory, or they do not believe that customer service can be measured effectively. There are, however, a few ways to measure the level of service that a consulting organization provides to its clients.

Quantitative research among current and former clients. It is possible to hire an outside market research organization to conduct interviews with current and former clients to determine the relative effectiveness of the customer service that one provides. This can be an excellent way to measure the service component of the business, but it is both expensive and time-consuming.

Implementation of exit interviews with clients at the completion of assignments. Some organizations measure the effectiveness of their customer service programs by interviewing people in the client organization on a one-to-one basis immediately after the conclusion of an assignment. At this point in the relationship, neither party has much to lose by this type of discussion, so the client personnel can be candid, and the consultant representatives can listen and ask questions to learn as much as possible about the reasons for the client views.

Ongoing discussions with key client personnel. This part of the measurement process should be employed regularly to give the management of the consulting organization feedback regarding the effectiveness of the entire customer service effort. It is desirable to begin a program of this nature with a specific outline of what elements of service the consultant wishes to explore with the client organization, to ensure that the discussion covers the most important points. Then, at the conclusion of the discussion, the consultant should write a brief memorandum that summarizes the key points in the discussion, including both positive and negative feedback.

SUMMARY

Effective customer service is vital to any successful consulting practice. The execution of a customer service program need not be difficult, if the appropriate strategy is developed and the people in the consulting organization have a commitment to the concept. Further, unlike many other aspects of the consultant's marketing mix, good customer service does not have to be costly or time-consuming. It simply requires a desire to meet the goals and a willingness to take the actions necessary to reach them.

14 The Ethics of the Consulting Business

One of the biggest reasons I have remained in the consulting business for so long is that it is possible for an individual (or organization) to operate in a highly ethical manner without getting involved in any gray areas. The ethics of the consulting business have always been important to me, because I need to be able to walk away from situations with clients that simply do not feel right, from a purely ethical or moral point of view, even when nothing illegal is involved.

For example, several years ago, I was hired by a client ostensibly to evaluate the grocery trade's reaction to a recently introduced product line. Throughout the assignment, there were constant references to a very unfriendly competitor, who my client felt was involved in illegal activities involving methods of gaining and maintaining distribution. What I did not know was that the client organization was preparing a major lawsuit against this competitor—this was announced shortly after the completion of our assignment—and the hidden agenda for our assignment (of which we were completely unaware) was for us to turn up evidence against the competitive organization that our client could use in its lawsuit.

When we presented the final report to the client, our conclusions and recommendations met with virtually no reaction. We had developed what we believed to be a very meaningful analysis of the product introduction and a strong action plan for business building; we had not, however, included any material that would help our client in the legal action. The client was upset.

Our client contacts asked us if we had uncovered any evidence of unusual or illegal practices on the part of the competition, but the objective of our work was not to explore that issue but to identify ways to make the client's business larger and more profitable. They then asked that we return to our field work to explore the area of their basic interest. What they wanted was not illegal, but we felt that it was unethical. Aside from the fact that it went against our own personal standards for the type of work we wanted to do, it would have required that we go back under false pretenses to the people whom we had already interviewed. The net of the situation was that we terminated our relationship with the client and had a very difficult time getting paid for the work we did.

This is an excellent example of a situation where ethics became significantly more important than financial considerations. I have never had second thoughts about the case, even though we have never again worked for that organization or any of the senior people who were involved in the project.

The ethics of the consulting business are really a two-way street. There are the ethics of the consultant, as they relate to the client—what most people would talk about if they were asked about the ethics of the consulting business. However, a second aspect of consulting ethics is also extremely important: the client's ethics in regard to the consultant.

It would be presumptuous of me to try to establish a code of ethics for the consulting profession, and, indeed, many of the specialized trade associations already have attempted to do this. However, I have found the existing standards to be so general that they have very little meaning to a great many consultants, particularly persons who are starting out in the business. This final chapter is intended to sensitize consultants to the ethical responsibilities of their practices and to identify several aspects of ethical practices that clients should follow with regard to their involvement with consultants.

ETHICS AND THE CONSULTANT

Honesty

Honesty is probably the ethical notion that is most important to the majority of people practicing consulting. I have always felt that most people are basically honest but, occasionally, succumb to temptation and do something questionable. Who has not received too much change from a cashier and decided not to say anything about it? Who has not found a little money, a nice pen, or another item of small value and kept it rather than trying to find the owner? These are not the types of dishonesty that I wish to deal with in this book. While I cannot condone it, it would be naive to make a fuss over these very minor infringements.

I feel that honesty in the consultant professions is vital in four areas.

Expenses.   Many (if not most) consultants establish working arrangements with their clients that call for fees plus expenses. Expenses should be defined at out-of-pocket costs incurred in the course of executing a consulting assignment for a client; they are not an opportunity for profit.

If your office is in New York and you have client business in California, it is clear that the client should pay your transportation costs to the West Coast and back. If you were seeing two clients during your visit, the ethical action would be to share the costs that are incurred between the two organizations so that they would each save money; however, some people would charge them both full price and so make money on the deal. This area of expenses represents a key ethical issue in the consulting business. My strong feeling is that the costs in this situation must be divided and that both clients should benefit from the cost savings, rather than you making money on the trip.

A very controversial ethical issue in consulting relates to the kinds of costs you incur. When you travel, what class of airline ticket do you purchase? What type of hotel do you stay in? How much money can you spend on meals? I have found that the airfare issue can be resolved either by writing into the contract that one will fly first class or explaining to clients the organization's policy with regard to this matter. About hotels,

I have had few problems, although, occasionally, a client has a policy regarding the amount that its executives can spend on rooms. You might find it advisable to check with the client contact before you book your first reservations, just to verify that you will not violate any company principles. This brief phone call can save you a lot of problems later on. Finally, with regard to meals, I always advise new consultants simply to use good judgement. Just because you are using someone else's money does not mean you can order a $35 bottle of wine, a flaming desert, and an after-dinner drink. If you are with clients and they want to order this, it is fine, but you should use great discretion about this type of overage when you are in control of the situation.

In the end, the ethics of expenses can be summed up quite easily: Consultants should incur only those expenses that are absolutely necessary and should report only those amounts.

Billing. Many consulting assignments are billed by the hour or by the day. In both cases, the consultant has an opportunity to bill extra to make up for any inefficiencies of the day. A key ethical principle that I feel must be a part of the culture of all consultants is to bill clients only for the work that has been done, even if the day (or week) has not been as productive as one would have liked. To do otherwise would be both dishonest and very unethical. Honesty in billing is a vital part of an effective consultant-client relationship.

Capabilities. Consultants should always be honest about their capabilities. Often, consultants are asked by a prospective client if they can be of help in an area in which they have no real expertise. It is very difficult to turn down business, particularly when things are slow, and consultants may figure that they can do the assignment reasonably well and the client will probably never know the difference. This is not an honest approach.

When client organizations hire consultants, they assume that the capabilities and expertise that they were told existed are in fact there, and they purchase the services based on that understanding. For consultants to undertake assignments that they do not feel they had the expertise to perform properly would be a violation of ethics. It would also probably be a very bad business decision, since the end result of the consulting assignment is unlikely to be a quality product that will generate additional revenues from future engagements.

Advice. I feel very strongly that clients pay for objective advice from the consultant and that is what they should receive, regardless of the apparent consequences. Over the years, I have been involved in many situations where we knew that the correct advice would not sit well with the client and probably would result in our not being retained for future assignments. In every case, I have felt strongly that we must tell our clients what is best for their business, even if it resulted in their dissatisfaction. This, in my judgement, is one of the most important parts of the consultant's ethic. Consultants should never change the advice they give to their clients in order to foster their own relationship with the organization. They should tell the clients what they should hear, even if it results in the loss of the consulting relationship.

Confidentiality

Confidentiality is probably the ethical area that is raised most often by clients at the start of a consulting relationship. It involves both internal and external issues.

Internal confidentiality. The nature of a consulting relationship demands that the consultant frequently communicate with various people throughout the client organization. It is vital that you accept the ethical responsibility that all conversations with client personnel remain confidential, much as in a doctor-patient environment, unless you have stated otherwise to the interviewee. Unless information is life threatening to someone in the organization, you should hold very fast to the confidentiality that you promised if management seeks to find out exactly who expressed what has been reported.

Another key aspect of internal confidentiality involves the practice of carrying stories from department to department. A consultant can do excessive damage to an organization if he or she reveals to one department what another has said.

While these principles may appear to be very obvious, my experience is that violating them can create real problems for a consultant. Some consultants have a tendency to want to show people in the client organization how well connected they are with senior management by relaying information about problems or issues in other departments or at the corporate level. This practice must be avoided, as it could destroy the entire consulting relationship.

External confidentiality. A major part of the consultant's ethic relates to confidentiality of information. Organizations that hire consultants are generally very concerned that the information they give to an outsider will slip into the hands of the competition. As a general rule, consultants should assume that all information they receive about client organizations should remain confidential indefinitely. There is no reason ever to share proprietary data about one organization with another.

One issue that frequently arises about confidentiality has to do with when a consultant can legitimately work for another company that is in competition with a former client. There is no established standard for this, and it normally is a function of the personal ethic of the consultant. As a general rule, most consultants feel comfortable working for a competitive company six to twelve months after completing an assignment for a client in the same business. This time frame will vary based on many different factors, such as the nature of the consulting practice, the extent of the original assignment, and the type of client.

Conflicts

Closely related to the area of confidentiality is the subject of competitive conflicts. A competitive conflict is generally defined as a situation where a consultant is working for two companies that are competing with each other. In virtually all aspects of consulting, this practice is frowned upon as being highly unethical. A consultant should establish a reputation for responsibility about competitive conflicts and should never work on an assignment where even a hint of competitive conflict exists.

All consultants should develop a written competitive conflict policy that identifies specifically what they define as a conflict. This document should be constructed in such a way that a potential competitive conflict can be resolved simply by identifying the issues and evaluating them against the policy. As a general rule, I have always defined a competitive conflict as a situation in which a consultant is working for two companies that are directly competitive with each other in the same product categories and the same locale. In essence, if the consultant's efforts with one company can have a negative impact on the success of another, then a conflict exists.

Consultants should rigorously adhere to their competitive conflict policies. It is very important for the consultant to tell prospective clients when he or she cannot work for them because of a competitive conflict. I find it useful in some situations to share the statement of competitive conflict with affected clients or prospects, so that they understand the importance you place on this issue.

Research

Often, a project requires the consultant to learn a good deal about the competition in the category, and there are many different ways of obtaining this information. Some consultants gain access to confidential information by pretending that they are writing an article for a trade journal or doing a master's (or doctor's) thesis; others conduct false job interviews with people from competitive companies for the purpose of gathering proprietary information. These are two of the most common unethical practices in the consulting business.

I feel very strongly that no consultant should undertake any research without revealing who he or she actually represents. A consultant can learn about a competitive company in many totally acceptable ways. To misrepresent oneself is both unethical and illegal and should be avoided at all costs.

Hiring Client Personnel

In the course of executing consulting assignments, consultants often develop close personal relationships with people from client organizations. In these situations, it is not unusual for consultants to feel that a particular client person would make a good addition to their organization, particularly in light of the individual's familiarity with the client company. However, it is a very bad idea for a consultant to hire anyone from a client company. There is almost no circumstance in which a client will condone consultants taking people away to work in their own organizations. When this happens, the consultant-client relationship inevitably will be damaged or terminated.

If consultants hire people from client organizations, they may also jeopardize their chances of obtaining future assignments from other companies. If a consultant has the reputation for hiring the best people from his or her client companies, a prospective client will think twice before hiring this individual.

Summary

The five key points of the consultant's ethic are summarized below:

- Honesty is essential in all aspects of the consultant-client relationship—billing, expenses, indications of capabilities, and advice to the client organization.

- Confidentiality is paramount in a consultant-client relationship. Never share information within the client organization or with others outside the client company.

- Consultants should adhere to a strict standard of exclusivity, never putting themselves in the position of working for two companies that can affect each other by virtue of the consultant's efforts.

- When doing research, consultants should never misrepresent themselves for the purpose of obtaining information that they otherwise would have been unable to secure.

- Never hire client personnel. This cannot help the relationship between the consultant and her client and it is not the type of action for which one wants to gain a reputation.

ETHICS AND THE CLIENT

If relatively little has appeared in the literature about ethical standards for the consultant, nothing of which I am aware has addressed the question of client ethics. Yet, just as the consultant is bound to operate under a very ethical standard, there are some very important ethics by which clients should abide, as they, too, have a responsibility in the relationship.

Payment on Time

Aside from the numerous legal/contractual reasons for prompt payment of bills, in my judgment, clients have an ethical responsibility to pay their consultants on time for services rendered. Unfortunately, many companies do not accept this responsibility because of internal desires to maximize cash flow. However, in many (if not most) situations, consulting practices are small businesses in comparison to the client organization, and reliable cash flow is absolutely crucial to the effective operations of the business. A payment received 30 or 60 days late can have a dramatic impact on a consultant's financial situation, whereas the client organization would not even miss it.

Honesty about the Objective of the Consulting Assignment

It is highly unethical for a client organization to have a hidden agenda when hiring a consultant. A consultant needs to be confident that the stated purpose of the assignment represents the real reason they have been engaged.

Respect for the Consultant's Time:

One of the biggest complaints of consultants is that client organizations use their financial power to take advantage of them. For example,

- A client organization may ask several different consultants for proposals for a potential consulting assignment, even though the management already knows that only one or two consultants that have been already identified will be considered. Often, this happens simply because company policy requires several bids. Most of the consultants have no chance of getting the assignment, but the client still asks them to take the time to develop a proposal.

- Some client organizations ask consultants to come in to discuss a problem and how the consultant could help resolve it, when all they really want is some free assistance.

- Too often, a consultant writes a very good proposal, but the client contact person wishes to use another consultant for personal reasons. The contact may go so far as to allow the favored candidate to copy the other's proposal and submit it with a somewhat lower cost, thus winning the assignment.

- Finally, some client organizations do not respect the boundaries of the client-consultant relationship and solicit assistance (at no cost) from the consultant in areas that are beyond the scope of the project. The client may ask casually whether the consultant can take a few minutes to review something of interest to the client or describe the extra help as a real quickie with which help would be appreciated.

Clients should respect the boundaries of the relationship and recognize that the only products the consultant has to sell are time and expertise and that one of the products—time—is a precious commodity. A client should never request a proposal under false pretenses and, if extra work is desired, it should be ready to pay for it.

Assistance and Information as Needed

Most consulting assignments require the involvement of people from the client organization—to supply information, schedule appointments, and so on. It is essential that client managements understand their ethical responsibilities to furnish the assistance that was promised to the consultant at the time the original proposal was approved. Often, the client organization gets busy with the day-to-day activities of running the business and does not provide the necessary support of the consultant or provides it very late and still expects the consultant to meet the project deadlines. This is damaging to both parties: The consultant cannot perform at his or her best, and the client organization does not get the optimum effort from the consultant.

Summary

The four key points of client ethics may be summarized as follows:

- Consultants should be paid in full and on time for the work they perform. Client companies should be aware of the cash flow implications of slow payments for consulting companies.

- Client companies should be completely honest with consultants relative to the purposes of their assignments.

- Client companies should be careful of their consultants' time and expertise and should not use their financial power to take advantage of either.

- Client organizations should do whatever they can to fulfill their responsibilities relative to providing any assistance promised in the proposal that the consultant needs to complete the assignment.

Index

Made in the USA
Lexington, KY
26 February 2015